GERMAN Verbs & Essentials of Grammar

Second Edition

Charles J. James

New York Chicago San Francisco Lisbon London Madrid Mexico City
Milan New Delhi San Juan Seoul Singapore Sydney Toronto

The McGraw Hill Companies

Copyright © 2008 by The McGraw-Hill Companies, Inc. All rights reserved. Printed in the United States of America. Except as permitted under the United States Copyright Act of 1976, no part of this publication may be reproduced or distributed in any form or by any means, or stored in a database or retrieval system, without the prior written permission of the publisher.

3 4 5 6 7 8 9 10 11 12 13 14 15 16 17 18 19 20 DSH/DSH 0

ISBN 978-0-07-184137-5

McGraw-Hill books are available at special quantity discounts to use as premiums and sales promotions or for use in corporate training programs. To contact a representative, please visit the Contact Us pages at www.mhprofessional.com.

This book is printed on acid-free paper.

Preface

German Verbs and Essentials of Grammar presents to its users the major grammatical concepts of the German language. The book is divided into two parts. In Part I, the major emphasis is placed on the mastery of verbs—their formation and uses, as well as their interconnections with other parts of speech. A chapter devoted to the most common verb prefixes reveals the creative ways in which the German language generates new words. The final chapter of Part I summarizes all the major verb tenses. All the chapters in this section provide numerous examples that highlight the forms and uses of German verbs in a meaningful context. Part II of this book offers concise explanations of the essential parts of German grammar—from the use of the article to rules of sentence formation that are characteristic of the German language. The final chapter of Part II features extensive vocabulary lists, each one related to the activities or objects of everyday life.

Examples illustrating grammar concepts were chosen for their authenticity, their frequency in everyday speech and writing, and their idiomatic quality. Each topic is treated separately, so that users of the book can either work on one topic at a time *or* quickly find the reference needed to help solve a particular difficulty. The table of the principal parts of common German verbs should prove an especially useful reference tool. Such tables provide ample material for creative exercises and extended writing, as well as for oral practice. In addition, the pronunciation section at the beginning of the book provides a helpful key to the main characteristics of the German sound system.

German Verbs and Essentials of Grammar is a valuable handbook that lends itself to a variety of uses. Because its basic approach is to provide simple, concise explanations, it can be used by language learners at all levels of proficiency—from those who have completed one semester's work to those who have attained a high level of mastery but who, from time to time, need a convenient reference to consult on difficult points of grammar. *German Verbs and Essentials of Grammar* can be used for study and review, for individual or group work, as part of a refresher course, or for business, travel, or research.

An excellent complement to this book is *Klett's Modern German and English Dictionary,* which contains an expanded listing of verb forms, guidelines for pronunciation, and abundant examples of the idioms most frequently encountered in contemporary German speech and writing. Other German dictionaries and language references available from Passport Books are listed at the end of this text.

Part One:
German Verbs

Part Two: Essentials of Grammar

18. The Article	63
19. Nouns	64
20. Prepositions	69
21. Adjectives and Adverbs	73
22. Numbers	78
23. Demonstrative Adjectives	82
24. Possessive Adjectives and Pronouns	84
25. Object Pronouns	85
26. Reflexive Pronouns	87
27. Relative Pronouns	89
28. Negatives	91
29. Interrogatives and Exclamations	93
30. Practical Sentence Rules	94
31. Suffixes	97
32. Time	98
33. Vocabulary Lists	101
Index	117
Verb Index	121

Contents

Part One: German Verbs

1. Pronunciation	3
2. Subject Pronouns	6
3. Present Tense—Regular Verbs	7
4. Present Tense—Irregular Verbs	12
5. Present Tense—Modal Verbs	14
6. Future	16
7. Preterite (Simple Past) Tense—Weak Verbs	17
8. Preterite Tense—Strong Verbs	19
9. Preterite Tense—Modal Verbs and Mixed Verbs	21
10. Past Participles and the Present Perfect Tense	23
11. Other Perfect Tenses	28
12. Verb Prefixes	30
13. The Imperative	34
14. Present Tense of the Subjunctive	36
15. Past Tense of the Subjunctive	40
16. The Passive Voice	41
17. Summary of Verb Forms	44

1. Pronunciation

The Alphabet

The German alphabet contains 26 letters. In addition, there are the three *umlaut* letters *ä, ö,* and *ü,* and the so-called *scharfes s* ("sharp s"), ß. These four letters are not part of the basic alphabet, although they are treated like letters in every other way. Letters of the alphabet are all neuter in gender *(das).*

The symbols between brackets ([ ]) indicate the pronunciation of the German names for the letters as rendered by the International Phonetic Alphabet.

a	[aː]	i	[iː]	q	[kuː]	y	[ʏpsilɔn]
b	[beː]	j	[jɔt]	r	[er]	z	[tsɛt]
c	[tseː]	k	[kaː]	s	[ɛs]	ß	[ɛstsɛt]
d	[deː]	l	[ɛl]	t	[teː]	ä	[eː]
e	[eː]	m	[ɛm]	u	[uː]	ö	[øː]
f	[ɛf]	n	[ɛn]	v	[faʊ]	ü	[yː]
g	[geː]	o	[oː]	w	[veː]		
h	[haː]	p	[peː]	x	[ɪks]		

[ː] The previous vowel is long.
['] The following syllable is stressed.
[ˌ] The following syllable has secondary stress (rare).
[ʔ] The so-called "glottal stop" (rare).
[-] In a series of syllables represents each individual syllable; in a partial transcription represents the remainder of the word.

Großes A capital A   *kleines a* small a

The English equivalents are given as guidelines to pronunciation, not as exact correspondents. Where no English equivalent is given, the sound and its spelling are close enough in both English and German to cause no significant pronunciation difficulties.

Vowels

[i]	bieten	['biːtən]	like English *ee* in *bee*
	zivil	[tsi'viːl]	
[ɪ]	bitten	['bɪtən]	like English *i* in *bit*
[e]	beten	['beːtən]	like English *ay* in *bay*
	wehren	['veːrən]	

[ɛ]	betten	['bɛtən]	like English *e* in *bet*
	währen	['vɛ:rən]	
[a]	Maat	[ma:t]	like English *o* in *not*
	wahren	['va:rən]	
	banal	[ba'na:l]	
[o]	Ofen	['of:ən]	like English *oa* in *boat*
	Ozon	[o'tso:n]	
[ɔ]	offen	['ɔfən]	like English *ou* in *bought* but much shorter!
[ø]	Öfen *pl*	['ø:fən]	like English *ir* in *girl* but without the *r*
	Höhle	['hølə]	
[œ]	öffnen	['œfnən]	like German [ø] but shorter
	Hölle	['hœlə]	
[u]	Pute	['pu:tə]	like English *oo* in *boot*
	zumute	[tsu'mu:tə]	
[ʊ]	Putte	['pʊtə]	like English *u* in *put*
	Mutter	['mʊtɐ]	
[y]	Tüte	['ty:tə]	like German *i* and *u* pronounced together
[ʏ]	Hütte	[hʏtə]	like German [y] but shorter
[ɐ]	aber	['a:bɐ]	vocalic *r*
	Ruhr	[ru:ɐ]	
[ə]	beleben	[bə'le.bən]	like English *e* in *butter*
[aɪ]	mein	[maɪn]	like English *i* in *mine*
[aʊ]	Maus	[maʊs]	like English *ou* in *mouse*
[ɔɪ]	neu	[nɔɪ]	like English *oy* in *boy*
	Mäuse *pl*	['mɔɪzə]	
[ã]	Balance	[ba'lã:s]	like English (French) *an* in *nuance*
[õ]	Bonbon	[bõ'bõ:]	like French *on* in *bon*
[œ̃]	Parfum	[par'fœ̃:]	like French *um* in *parfum*
[ɛ̃]	Bassin	[ba'sɛ̃:]	like French *in* in *bassin*

Consonants

[b]	Bibel	['bi:bəl]	like English *b* in *baby*
[ç]	nicht	[nɪçt]	between English *sh* and *k*
	ächten	['eçtən]	
[x]	Nacht	[naxt]	behind English *k* but with mild friction
	achten	['axtən]	
[d]	doch	[dɔx]	like English *d* in *drum*
[f]	Frevel	['fre:fəl]	like English *f* in *fifty*
	Vielfalt	['fi:lfalt]	
[g]	gegen	[ge:gən]	always like English *g* in *go*
[ʒ]	Genie	[ʒe'ni:]	like second *g* in English *garage*
	Garage	[ga'ra:ʒə]	
[h]	Hahn	[ha:n]	like English *h* in *hat*
[j]	jagen	['ja:gən]	always like English *y* in *yes*
[k]	Krieg	[kri:k]	like English *k* in *keep*
	Knick	[knɪk]	
[l]	lallen	['lalən]	like English *l* in *lily*
	labil	[la'bi:l]	
[m]	Mumm	[mʊm]	like English *m* in *murmur*
[n]	nennen	['nɛnɛn]	like English *n* in *no*

[ŋ]	fangen	['faŋən]	always like *ng* in English *singer*
	denken	['dɛŋkən]	never like *ng* in English *finger*
[p]	Pappe	['papə]	like English *p* in *pepper*
[r]	Rohre *pl*	['ro:rə]	pronounced off the uvula in some varieties, trilled in others, never like English *r*
[s]	Mars	[mars]	like English *s* in *less*
	küssen	['kʏsən]	
	fließen	['fli:sən]	
[z]	Sense	['zɛnzə]	like English *z* in *zebra*
	sausen	['zauzən]	
[ʃ]	Schau	[ʃau]	like English *sh* in *she*
	stehlen	['ʃte:lən]	
	spielen	['ʃpi:lən]	
[t]	Tat	[ta:t]	like English *t* in *tie*
	Tod	[to:t]	
[ts]	Zoo	[tso:]	like English *ts* in *recruits*
	Zitze	[tsɪtse]	
[v]	Wein	[vaɪn]	like English *v* in *vivid*

Punctuation Marks

,	das Komma		( )	die runde(n) Klammer (n)
.	der Punkt		[ ]	die eckige(n) Klammer(n)
:	der Doppelpunkt		'	der Apostroph
;	der Strichpunkt		-	der Bindestrich
?	das Fragezeichen		—	der Gedankenstrich
!	das Ausrufungszeichen		" "	die Anführungsstriche

2. Subject Pronouns

	Singular			Plural	
1.	ich	I	1.	wir	we
2.	du	you	2.	ihr	you
	Sie	you		Sie	you
3.	er	he, it		sie	they
	sie	she, it			
	es	it			
	man	you, they, people, etc.			

Sie is the polite form of "you." It is used with strangers, superiors, professional colleagues, and others not well known to the speaker. *Sie* can be singular or plural in meaning, depending on context.

Herr und Frau Schmidt, können *Sie* es heute bringen?	Mr. and Mrs. Schmidt, can you bring it today?
Frau Eckert, haben *Sie* gerade angerufen?	Mrs. Eckert, did you just call?

Du is the familiar form of "you." Its plural is *ihr*. It is used when speaking to family members, children, close friends, animals, and deities.

Wohnst *du* schon lange hier, Martin?	Have you lived here long, Martin?
Wohnt *ihr* schon lange hier, Kinder?	Have you lived here long, children?

The subject pronoun *du* is also used pejoratively, when the speaker wishes to show superiority or contempt towards the person to whom he or she is speaking.

Du Feigling!	You coward!

Man corresponds to the English "one," "they," "people," or "you" when it is used without reference to a particular individual. It is very common in German, especially when the speaker wishes to describe an activity without indicating who is performing the activity.

Man *sagt*,...	They say,...
Man *sieht hier*...	You see here...
Man *hat behauptet*,...	It has been claimed,...

3. Present Tense—Regular Verbs

Infinitives

All German verbs have an infinitive ending in *-(e)n*. This is the form found in dictionaries.

rufen   to call
schlafen   to sleep

arbeiten   to work

The infinitive without the ending *-(e)n* is called the *stem*. Endings added to the stem indicate person, number, tense, and mood.

ruf*en*	er ruf*t*	he calls
schlaf*en*	sie schlaf*en*	they sleep
arbeit*en*	ich arbeit*ete*	I worked

The present tense expresses an ongoing action, general state, or habitual activity. It corresponds to all three English present tenses, as in

I write letters.
I am writing a letter now.
I do write letters well!

Forming the Present Tense

The present tense is formed by adding the following number and person endings to the stem.

	Singular			Plural	
1.	ich	*-e*	1.	wir	*-en*
2.	du	*-st*	2.	ihr	*-t*
	Sie	*-en*		Sie	*-en*
3.	man	*-t*	3.	sie	*-en*

machen, to do
I do, do do, am doing, you do, etc.

Singular			Plural	
1.	ich mach*e*	I do	1. wir mach*en*	we do
2.	du mach*st*	you do	2. ihr mach*t*	you do
	Sie mach*en*	you do	Sie mach*en*	you do
3.	er mach*t*	it, he does	3. sie mach*en*	they do
	sie mach*t*	it, she does		
	es mach*t*	it does		
	man mach*t*	people do		

Was machst du? What are you doing?
Ich mache meine Hausaufgabe. I am doing my homework.
Er macht alles falsch! He does everything wrong!
So (et)was macht man hier nicht! You don't do that sort of thing here!

Sample Verbs Conjugated in the Present Tense like *machen*

brauchen	to need	**lernen**	to learn
bringen	to bring	**lieben**	to love
denken	to think	**liegen**	to lie, to recline
drucken	to print	**rufen**	to call someone
drücken	to press, to push	**sagen**	to say
fragen	to ask someone	**schicken**	to send
führen	to lead, to guide	**singen**	to sing
gehen	to go	**sitzen**	to sit
heißen	to be called	**spielen**	to play
holen	to fetch, to get something	**stehen**	to stand
hören	to hear, to listen	**stellen**	to put something into a vertical position
kaufen	to buy		
kennen	to know somebody	**suchen**	to look for
kochen	to cook, to boil	**trinken**	to drink
kommen	to come	**wohnen**	to live somewhere
lachen	to laugh	**zeigen**	to show
leben	to live, to be alive		
legen	to put something into a horizontal position		

Most verbs in German form their present tense like the verbs above.

Verb Stems ending in -t(-), -d(-), or -gn(-)

Verbs whose stem ends in *-t*(-), *-d*(-), *-d*(-) or *-gn*(-) usually add an *-e*(-) before attaching the endings *-st* and *-t*.

arbeiten, to work
I work, do work, am working, etc.

Singular
1. **ich arbeite**   I work
2. **du arbeitest**   you work
   Sie arbeiten   you work
3. **er arbeitet**   he works
   sie arbeitet   she works
   es arbeitet   it works
   man arbeitet   people work

Plural
1. **wir arbeiten**   we work
2. **ihr arbeitet**   you work
   Sie arbeiten   you work
3. **sie arbeiten**   they work

Ich arbeite Tag und Nacht.   I work day and night.
Wo arbeitet Ihre Frau?   Where does your wife work?
Sie arbeitet bei einer Bank.   She works at a bank.

Sample Verbs Conjugated in the Present Tense like *arbeiten*

antworten   to answer
bieten   to offer
binden   to tie
bitten   to request, to ask for
finden   to find
heiraten   to marry
leiden   to suffer

leisten   to accomplish
leiten   to direct
melden   to report in
reden   to give a speech
regnen   to rain
schneiden   to cut
toten   to kill

Stem-Vowel Change Verbs

A number of common verbs change the vowel in their stem in the second person singular informal (*du*) and third person singular forms (*er, sie,* or *man*). The pattern of change is as follows:

  a becomes ä
  au becomes äu
  e becomes ie or i
  o becomes ö

Verbs with *u* in the stem do not undergo this change.

geben, to give
I give, do give, am giving, etc.

Singular
1. **ich gebe**   I give
2. **du g*i*bst**   you give
   Sie geben   you give
3. **er g*i*bt**   he gives
   sie g*i*bt   she gives
   es g*i*bt   it gives
   man g*i*bt   people give

Plural
1. **wir geben**   we give
2. **ihr gebt**   you give
   Sie geben   you give
3. **sie geben**   they give

Gibst du mir das Geld?   Are you giving me the money?
Er gibt dir das Geld.   He gives you the money.

sehen, to see
I see, do see, am seeing, etc.

Singular			Plural		
1.	ich sehe	I see	1.	wir sehen	we see
2.	du s*ieh*st	you see	2.	ihr seht	you see
	Sie sehen	you see		Sie sehen	you see
3.	er s*ieh*t	he sees	3.	sie sehen	they see
	sie s*ieh*t	she sees			
	es s*ieh*t	it sees			
	man s*ieh*t	people see			

Ich sehe, was du nicht siehst.   I see what you don't see.
Man sieht die Sterne mit dem bloßen Augen.   You (can) see the stars with the naked eye.

tragen, to wear, to carry
I wear, carry, am wearing, am carrying, etc.

Singular			Plural		
1.	ich trage	I wear	1.	wir tragen	we wear
2.	du trägst	you wear	2.	ihr tragt	you wear
	Sie tragen	you wear		Sie tragen	you wear
3.	er trägt	he wears	3.	sie tragen	they wear
	sie trägt	she wears			
	es trägt	it wears			
	man trägt	people wear			

Ein Deutscher trägt selten Lederhosen.   A German rarely wears *Lederhosen*.
Trägst du deine neue Uhr?   Are you wearing your new watch?
Ein Gepäckträger trägt Gepäck.   A porter carries baggage.

Sample Verbs with a Stem-Vowel Change

brechen (*bricht*)   to break
essen (*ißt*)   to eat
fahren (*fährt*)   to drive, to go
fallen (*fällt*)   to fall
empfehlen (*empfiehlt*)   to recommend
halten (*hält*)   to hold
laden (*lädt*)   to load
laufen (*läuft*)   to walk, to run
lesen (*liest*)   to read

schlafen (*schläft*)   to sleep
schlagen (*schlägt*)   to hit
sterben (*stirbt*)   to die
stossen (*stößt*)   to push
treten (*tritt*)   to step
vergessen (*vergißt*)   to forget
wachsen (*wächst*)   to grow
waschen (*wäscht*)   to wash

Negative Form

To form a negative verb statement, place *nicht* after the verb.

Es regnet *nicht.*	It does not rain./It is not raining.
Wir antworten *nicht.*	We do not answer./We are not answering.
Das Auto geht *nicht.*	The car does not work./The car isn't working.

See Chapter 28, **Negatives,** for a further discussion of the placement of *nicht*, as well as the use of other negatives, such as *kein, niemand, nie,* and *nichts.*

Interrogative Form

To form a question, simply place the subject after the verb. German does not use a form such as "do" or "does."

Sprechen Sie Deutsch?	Do you speak German?/Are you speaking German?
Schreibt dein Freund oft?	Does your friend write often?
Haben Sie Zeit?	Do you have time?

4. Present Tense— Irregular Verbs

1. There is only one genuinely irregular verb in German, *sein*.

   sein, to be
   I am, you are, it is, etc.

   Singular
   1. **ich bin**   I am
   2. **du bist**   you are
   3. **man ist*** one is

   Plural
   1. **wir sind**   we are
   2. **ihr seid**   you are
   3. **sie sind*** they are

   Ich bin Berliner.   I am a Berliner.
   Wir sind Amerikaner.   We are Americans.
   Ihr seid aber lieb.   You are really nice.
   Sie sind kindisch.   You (or they) are childish.

2. Three other very common verbs have forms which are slightly irregular, which is why they are listed here.

   haben, to have
   I have, you have, he has, etc.

   Singular
   1. **ich habe**   I have
   2. **du hast**   you have
   3. **man hat***   one has

   Plural
   1. **wir haben**   we have
   2. **ihr habt**   you have
   3. **sie haben*** they have

   Ich habe ein Buch.   I have a book.
   Man hat selten Zeit.   You rarely have time.
   Ihr habt recht.   You are (*lit.* have) right.

   *Note: From now on the *Sie* ("you") forms of verbs will not be listed separately since they are *exactly* the same as the third person plural form of *sie*. Also, the *er, sie, es* ("he," "she," "it") forms will be illustrated by the pronoun *man* hereafter.

wissen, to know (a fact)
I know, you know, she knows, etc.

Singular
1. **ich weiß**   I know
2. **du weißt**   you know
3. **man weiß**   one knows

Plural
1. **wir wissen**   we know
2. **ihr wißt**   you know
3. **sie wissen**   they know

Wissen Sie, wer ich bin?   Do you know who I am?
Nein, ich weiß nicht, wer Sie sind!   No, I don't know who you are!
Viele wissen, was Sie nicht wissen.   Many (people) know, what you don't know.

werden, to become, to get, to turn, to change
I become, you become, they become, etc.

Singular
1. **ich werde**   I become
2. **du wirst**   you become
3. **man wird**   one becomes

Plural
1. **wir werden**   we become
2. **ihr werdet**   you become
3. **sie werden**   they become

Das Wetter wird besser.   The weather is getting better.
Ich werde älter.   I am getting older.
Ihr Gesicht wird grün.   Her (your, their) face is turning green.
Ich werde langsam ungeduldig!   I am slowly becoming impatient!

5. Present Tense— Modal Verbs

Modal verbs, also called *modal auxiliaries* (German *Modalverben*), express the ideas of permission, obligation, etc. Their plural forms are regular. Their singular forms, however, exhibit certain irregularities.

können, to be able to
I can, am able to, etc.

Singular
1. ich kann
2. du kannst
3. man kann

Plural
1. wir können
2. ihr könnt
3. sie können

sollen, to be supposed to
I should, ought to, am supposed to, etc.

Singular
1. ich soll
2. du sollst
3. man soll

Plural
1. wir sollen
2. ihr sollt
3. sie sollen

müssen, to have to
I must, have to, am obliged to, etc.

Singular
1. ich muß
2. du mußt
3. man muß

Plural
1. wir müssen
2. ihr müßt
3. sie müssen

wollen, to want to
I want to, you want to, etc.

Singular
1. ich will
2. du willst
3. man will

Plural
1. wir wollen
2. ihr wollt
3. sie wollen

dürfen, to be allowed to
I may, am allowed, have permission to, etc.

Singular
1. ich darf
2. du darfst
3. man darf

Plural
1. wir dürfen
2. ihr dürft
3. sie dürfen

mögen, to like (to)
I like (to), etc.

Singular
1. ich mag
2. du magst
3. man mag

Plural
1. wir mögen
2. ihr mögt
3. sie mögen

Modals are used with the infinitive of a verb that expresses the main idea of a clause or sentence. The infinitive stands at the end of the clause or sentence in question.

Ich schreibe Briefe.	I write letters.
Ich muß Briefe schreiben.	I have to write letters./I must write letters.
Er geht jetzt nach Hause.	He is going home now.
Er will jetzt nach Hause gehen.	He wants to go home now.
Wir besuchen den Gefangenen.	We are visiting the prisoner.
Wir dürfen den Gefangenen besuchen.	We are allowed to visit the prisoner.

6. Future

1. The future is expressed in German in two ways. First of all, it is expressed by the present tense with appropriate time markers.

Ich komme *morgen*.	I'll come tomorrow.
Wir fahren *nächste Woche* **nach Australien.**	We'll be going to Australia next week.
Er bringt es *gleich zurück*.	He'll bring it right back.

2. Secondly, there is a future tense that is formed by using the present tense of *werden* plus the infinitive of the verb in question. Note that *werden* operates exactly like a modal auxiliary.

   machen to do, to make

ich *werde*...**machen**	I will do	**wir** *werden*...**machen**	we will do
du *wirst*...**machen**	you will do	**ihr** *werdet*...**machen**	you will do
man *wird*...**machen**	people will do	**sie** *werden*...**machen**	they will do

Ich werde morgen kommen.	I'll come tomorrow.
Wir werden nächste Woche nach Australien fahren.	We'll be going to Australia next week.
Er wird es gleich zurückbringen.	He'll bring it right back.

   The future tense is not used as often in German as it is in English.

7. Preterite (Simple Past) Tense—Weak Verbs

German verbs have two sets of past tense forms: the preterite (or simple past) and the present perfect. For all practical purposes their meaning is the same. Both sets of past tense forms have all the meanings found in the English verb forms "I wrote," "I was writing," "I have written," or "I did write."

Preterite:	**Ich schrieb.**	I wrote. / I was writing.
Present Perfect:	**Ich habe geschrieben.**	I did write. / I have written.

It is possible to find *both* past tense forms in the same text or conversation. The differences between the two are regional and stylistic; describing them goes beyond the scope of this book.

Formation of the Preterite

There are two large groups of verbs based on the formation of their preterite tense forms. The groups are frequently labeled *weak* and *strong*. These labels are interesting only from a historical point of view.

Verbs like *machen* are weak verbs. To form their preterite, simply take the stem, add *-te* and then attach the following endings:

ich	—	wir	-n
du	-st	ihr	-t
man	—	sie	-n

machen, to do, to make
I did, was doing, did do, have done, etc.

ich mach*te*	I did	**wir mach*ten***	we did
du mach*test*	you did	**ihr mach*tet***	you did
man mach*te*	people did	**sie mach*ten***	they did

Weak verbs are sometimes also called *regular verbs*.

Sample Verbs Conjugated in the Preterite Tense like *machen/machte*.

Infinitive		Preterite	
bauen	to build	**baute**	built
brauchen	to need	**brauchte**	needed
dauern	to last	**dauerte**	lasted
decken	to cover	**deckte**	covered
drücken	to press	**drückte**	pressed
fragen	to ask	**fragte**	asked
führen	to lead	**führte**	led
holen	to fetch	**holte**	fetched
hören	to hear	**hörte**	heard
kaufen	to buy	**kaufte**	bought
kochen	to cook	**kochte**	cooked
lachen	to laugh	**lachte**	laughed
lächeln	to smile	**lächelte**	smiled
lernen	to learn	**lernte**	learned
lieben	to love	**liebte**	loved
schauen	to look at	**schaute**	looked at
schicken	to send	**schickte**	sent
setzen	to set	**setzte**	set
spielen	to play	**spielte**	played
stören	to disturb	**störte**	disturbed
suchen	to look for	**suchte**	looked for
zeigen	to show	**zeigte**	showed

8. Preterite Tense— Strong Verbs

Verbs like *sehen* are *strong* verbs. They require a change in the stem vowel that is not always predictable. The same thing often happens in English: "see"—"saw," "do"—"did," "come"—"came," "go"—"went," "be"—"was," etc. The preterite (simple past) tense endings for strong verbs are the same as those for weak verbs such as *machen*.

ich	—	wir	-en
du	-st	ihr	-t
man	—	sie	-en

sehen, to see
I saw, was seeing, did see, have seen, etc.

ich sah	wir sahen
du sahst	ihr saht
man sah	sie sahen

Ich sah sie gestern.   I saw her yesterday.
Wir sahen den Film nicht.   We didn't see the film.

As with English irregular verbs, the vowel changes for strong verbs have to be memorized.

Sample Verbs Conjugated in the Preterite Tense like *sehen/sah*.

Infinitive		Preterite	
brechen	to break	brach	broke
fahren	to drive	fuhr	drove
fallen	to fall	fiel	fell
fangen	to catch	fing	caught
geben	to give	gab	gave
gehen	to go	ging	went
helfen	to help	half	helped
kommen	to come	kam	came
laufen	to run	lief	ran
liegen	to lie	lag	lay
lügen	to tell a lie	log	lied
nehmen	to take	nahm	took
pfeiffen	to whistle	pfiff	whistled

reissen	to tear	**riß**	tore
riechen	to smell	**roch**	smelled
rufen	to call	**rief**	called
schlafen	to sleep	**schlief**	slept
schlagen	to hit	**schlug**	hit
schreiben	to write	**schrieb**	wrote
singen	to sing	**sang**	sang
sprechen	to speak	**sprach**	spoke
stehen	to stand	**stand**	stood
steigen	to climb	**stieg**	climbed
sterben	to die	**starb**	died
tragen	to wear	**trug**	wore
trinken	to drink	**trank**	drank
werfen	to throw	**warf**	threw
ziehen	to pull	**zog**	pulled

Sein, Haben, and *Werden*

The verbs *sein, haben,* and *werden* have predictable preterite forms, but are listed here as further examples of the formation of the preterite.

sein, to be
I was, was being, have been, etc.

ich war	**wir waren**
du warst	**ihr wart**
man war	**sie waren**

Warst du gestern zu Hause? — Were you home yesterday?
Nein, ich war bei meiner Tante. — No, I was visiting (at) my aunt.

haben, to have
I had, was having, did have, have had, etc.

ich hatte	**wir hatten**
du hattest	**ihr hattet**
man hatte	**sie hatten**

Ich hatte einmal einen Hund. — I once had a dog.
Meine Schwester und ich hatten ihn sehr gern. — My sister and I liked him very much (*lit.* had him very gladly).

werden, to become
I became, was becoming, did become, have become, etc.

ich wurde	**wir wurden**
du wurdest	**ihr wurdet**
man wurde	**sie wurden**

Was wurden Ihre Eltern? — What did your parents become?
Meine Mutter wurde Ärztin und mein Vater wurde Pilot. — My mother became a physician and my father became a pilot.

9. Preterite Tense—Modal Verbs and Mixed Verbs

The Preterite of Modal Verbs

Some modal verbs have an irregular stem in the preterite, but *all* modals have a regular (*-te*) past tense marker. Note that the preterite (simple past) tense endings for modals are the same as those for weaker verbs (see page 17).

können, to be able to
I was able to, could, you were able to, you could, etc.

ich konnte	wir konnten
du konntest	ihr konntet
man konnte	sie konnten

Ich konnte es kaum glauben!	I could hardly believe it!
Wir konnten es uns nicht leisten.	We couldn't afford it.
Das konnte man klar sehen.	You could see that clearly.

sollen, to be supposed to
I was supposed to, ought to have (-ed), etc.

ich sollte	wir sollten
du solltest	ihr solltet
man sollte	sie sollten

Wir sollten gestern um die Zeit kommen.	We were supposed to come at that time yesterday.
Du solltest das wirklich sehen.	You really should have seen that.

müssen, to have to
I had to, was obliged to, etc.

ich mußte	wir mußten
du mußtest	ihr mußtet
man mußte	sie mußten

Ich mußte das machen.	I had to do that.
Wir mußten die Aufgabe nicht* machen.	We did not have to do the assignment.

*Note: *Nicht müssen* does not mean "must not."

wollen, to want to
I wanted to, you wanted to, etc.

ich wollte	wir wollten
du wolltest	ihr wolltet
man wollte	sie wollten

Du wolltest es mir schon lange sagen, nicht wahr?	You have wanted to tell me that for a long time, haven't you?
Ich wollte die Nachricht nicht glauben.	I didn't want to believe the report.
Wir wollten auf den Eiffel-Turm steigen.	We wanted to climb (up) the Eiffel Tower.

dürfen, to be allowed to
I was allowed to, had permission to, etc.

ich durfte	wir durften
du durftest	ihr durftet
man durfte	sie durften

Wir wollten ins Kino gehen, aber wir durften nicht.	We wanted to go to the movies, but we were not allowed to.
Ich durfte nicht zu Hause bleiben.	I was not allowed to stay home.

mögen, to like (to)
I liked to, you liked to, etc.

ich mochte	wir mochten
du mochtest	ihr mochtet
man mochte	sie mochten

Ich mochte die Farbe nicht.	I didn't like the color.
Sie mochten den Krimi im Fernsehen.	They liked the mystery film on television.

The Preterite of Mixed Verbs

In addition to the modal verbs, there are a number of common verbs, called *mixed verbs,* that form their preterite by changing the stem and adding *-te.* These verbs are *bringen, kennen, denken, rennen,* and *wissen. Wissen* is the most common of the mixed verbs and serves as a model for the others.

wissen, to know (a fact)
I knew, did know, have known, etc.

ich wußte	wir wußten
du wußtest	ihr wußtet
man wußte	sie wußten

Ich wußte es doch!	I did (too) know that!
Wir wußten nicht, wie lange es dauern sollte.	We didn't know how long it was supposed to last.

10. Past Participles and the Present Perfect Tense

1. German has three perfect tenses: the present perfect *(Perfekt)*, past perfect *(Plusquamperfekt)*, and future perfect *(Futurum Perfekt)*. The perfect tenses are also called "compound tenses." Only the present perfect is used extensively.

2. The present perfect is formed by using the past participle plus the present tense of either *haben* or *sein*.

Er *hat* **in Paris** *gewohnt*.   He lived in Paris.
Wir *sind* **ins Kino** *gegangen*.   We went to the movies.

The past participle of weak verbs is formed by taking the stem of the verb, adding *-t* to the end, and prefixing *ge-*.

machen to do   *gemacht* done

Other verbs like *machen* form their past participle exactly the same way. Here are some of the most common.

Infinitive		Past Participle	
bauen	to build	**gebaut**	built
decken	to cover	**gedeckt**	covered
fragen	to ask	**gefragt**	asked
hören	to hear	**gehört**	heard
kaufen	to buy	**gekauft**	bought
lachen	to laugh	**gelacht**	laughed
lernen	to learn	**gelernt**	learned
lieben	to love	**geliebt**	loved
sagen	to say, tell	**gesagt**	said, told
spielen	to play	**gespielt**	played
suchen	to look for	**gesucht**	looked for
zeigen	to show	**gezeigt**	showed

3. Verbs such as *antworten,* which add an -*e*(-) before attaching the endings -*st* and -*t* in the present, add an -*e*(-) before attaching the -*t* of the past participle.

antworten to answer **geantwortet** answered

Infinitive   Past Participle

arbeiten to work   **gearbeitet** worked
heiraten to get married   **geheiratet** got married
leisten   to accomplish   **geleistet**   accomplished
leiten   to conduct   **geleitet**   conducted
reden   to give a speech   **geredet**   given a speech
regnen   to rain   **geregnet**   rained
töten   to kill   **getötet**   killed

4. Strong verbs like *brechen* usually add -*en* instead of -*t* to the end of the past participle. In many strong verbs, there is also a change in the stem vowel.

brechen to break   **gebrochen** broken

Some other past participles of strong verbs include:

Infinitive   Past Participle

binden   to tie   **gebunden** tied
bleiben to stay   **geblieben** stayed
finden   to find   **gefunden** found
geben   to give   **gegeben**   given
lesen   to read   **gelesen**   read
rufen   to call   **gerufen**   called
werden   to become   **geworden** become

5. The following past participles have certain irregularities in their formation, but also end in -*en* and begin with *ge*-:

Infinitive   Past Participle

essen   to eat   **gegessen**   eaten
gehen   to go   **gegangen**   gone
nehmen to take   **genommen**   taken
sein   to be   **gewesen**   been
sitzen to sit   **gesessen**   sat
stehen to stand   **gestanden** stood

Past Participles without *ge-*

All verbs whose infinitive ends in -*ieren* form the past participle without the *ge-* prefix. Instead, they take the -*t* ending common to the past participles of weak verbs, which they all are.

Infinitive		Past Participle	
delegieren	to delegate	**delegiert**	delegated
interessieren	to interest	**interessiert**	interested
marschieren	to march	**marschiert**	marched
qualifizieren	to qualify	**qualifiziert**	qualified
regieren	to govern	**regiert**	governed
studieren	to study	**studiert**	studied

Note: All verbs ending in *-ieren* are weak verbs and form all their tenses according to the pattern of verbs such as *machen*.

Past Participles with Prefixes

1. Certain verb prefixes "preempt" the *ge-* participial prefix. The meanings and uses of these prefixes will be discussed in Chapter 12, **Verb Prefixes**. The prefixes in question are: *be-, emp-, ent-, er-, ge-, ver-,* and *zer-*. Examples include:

Infinitive		Past Participle	
besuchen	to visit	**besucht**	visited
empfehlen	to recommend	**empfohlen**	recommended
erleben	to experience	**erlebt**	experienced
gefallen	to please	**gefallen**	pleased
vergessen	to forget	**vergessen**	forgotten
zerstören	to destroy	**zerstört**	destroyed

2. Sometimes the following prefixes also override the *ge-* prefix: *durch-, um-, unter-,* and *über-*.

Infinitive		Past Participle	
durchsuchen	to search	**durchsucht**	searched
übersetzen	to translate	**übersetzt**	translated
umschreiben	to transcribe	**umschrieben**	transcribed
unterschreiben	to sign	**unterschrieben**	signed

3. Whether or not the participle will end in *-t* or *-en* depends upon the verb from which it is derived. If the verb with the prefix is taken from a weak verb, it will end in *-t*.

Infinitive		Past Participle	
bestellen	to order	**bestellt**	ordered
entsetzen	to horrify	**entsetzt**	horrified
versuchen	to try	**versucht**	tried

4. If the verb is taken from a strong verb, it will end in *-en*.

Infinitive		Past Participle	
bestehen	to pass	**bestanden**	passed (a test)
erfinden	to invent	**erfunden**	invented
verstehen	to understand	**verstanden**	understood

Forming the Present Perfect

The present perfect tense is usually formed by using the appropriate present tense form of *haben* and placing the past participle at the end of the clause or sentence.

Hast du das Buch *gekauft?*	Have you bought the book?
Ja, und ich *habe* das Buch auch *gelesen.*	Yes, and I have also read the book.
Habt ihr den Film *gesehen?*	Have you (all) seen the movie?
Ja, und wir *haben* den Film sehr lustig *gefunden.*	Yes, and we found the movie very funny.
Haben die Arbeiter die Brücke *errichtet?*	Have the workers erected the bridge?
Ja, aber der Chef *hat* die Arbeit nicht *genehmigt.*	Yes, but the boss did not approve the work.

Present Perfect with Modals

1. The modal verbs have "true" past participles. However, they are used only when they are "full" verbs, that is, when they are used without an infinitive.

Ich mag Leber nicht und habe sie nie *gemocht.*	I do not like liver and have never liked it.
Wir haben nicht *gewollt,* daß es zu einem Unfall kommen sollte.	We didn't want it to come to an accident.
Du kannst nicht tanzen und hast es nie *gekonnt.*	You cannot dance and never have been able to.

2. Otherwise, the infinitive is used where a past participle would be expected. It is placed after the infinitive of the main idea in the sentence.

Present:	**Ich kann schreiben.**	I can write.
Preterite:	**Ich konnte schreiben.**	I was able to write.
Present Perfect:	**Ich *habe* schreiben *können.***	I have been able to write./ I was able to write.
Present:	**Du darfst gehen.**	You may go.
Preterite:	**Du dürftest gehen.**	You were allowed to go.
Present Perfect:	**Du *hast* gehen *dürfen.***	You have been allowed to go./ You were allowed to go.

Note: The modals *all* take *haben* in the present perfect.

3. In the following list, the "true" past participles are given in parentheses:

können	to be able to	(gekonnt) **können**	been able to
dürfen	to be allowed to	(gedurft) **dürfen**	been allowed to
sollen	to be supposed to	(gesollt) **sollen**	been supposed to
müssen	to be obligated to	(gemußt) **müssen**	been obligated to
wollen	to want	(gewollt) **wollen**	wanted
mögen	to like (to)	(gemocht) **mögen**	liked (to)

The Present Perfect Tense with *sein*

A number of common verbs do not use the auxiliary verb *haben* to form their perfect tenses. Instead they use the corresponding forms of *sein*. Most are verbs of motion or being, including *sein* itself. Most of them, in addition, happen to be strong verbs as well.

Ist Herr Braun zu Hause geblieben?   Did Mr. Braun stay at home?
Bist du in die Stadt gefahren?   Did you drive into the city?

Verbs that commonly use *sein* in compound tenses include:

Infinitive		Present Perfect (third person singular)	
bleiben	to stay	**ist geblieben**	stayed
fahren	to go by vehicle	**ist gefahren**	gone by vehicle
fallen	to fall	**ist gefallen**	fallen
fliessen	to flow	**ist geflossen**	flowed
gehen	to go	**ist gegangen**	gone
kommen	to come	**ist gekommen**	come
reisen	to travel	**ist gereist**	traveled
sein	to be	**ist gewesen**	been
steigen	to climb	**ist gestiegen**	climbed
sterben	to die	**ist gestorben**	died
werden	to become	**ist geworden**	become

11. Other Perfect Tenses

The Past Perfect Tense

1. The past perfect is formed exactly like the present perfect except that the appropriate preterite form of *haben* or *sein* is used.

   Ich *hatte* das Buch *gelesen*. I had read the book.
   Wir *hatten* den Film *gesehen*. We had seen the movie.
   Wir *waren* schon *gekommen*. We had already come.

2. Usually the past perfect is used with one or more other past tenses, since it indicates an activity that occurred before some other activity in the past. The use of the past perfect is as rare in German as it is in English.

   Wir haben den Film gesehen, erst nachdem wir den Roman gelesen hatten. We saw the film only after we had read the novel.
   Es hat zu regnen angefangen, nachdem er angekommen war. It started to rain, after he had arrived.

The Future Perfect Tense

1. The future perfect is formed by using the present tense of *werden* plus the past participle with either *haben* or *sein* at the end of the clause, depending on the verb in question. Sentences in the future perfect in both English and German frequently contain a time expression such as *bis...* ("by...").

   Ich werde das Buch bis Montag gelesen haben. I will have read the book by Monday.
   Du wirst den Bericht bis dahin geschrieben haben. You will have written the report by then.
   Er wird bis nächstes Jahr umgezogen sein. He will have moved by next year.

2. German has a somewhat unusual use for its future perfect. Combined with the adverb *wohl* ("probably"), the future perfect refers to an event that *has probably already taken place,* although the speaker is not sure whether or not this is true.

Mein Sohn wird die Hausaufgaben *wohl* **gemacht haben.**	My son has (probably) already done his homework.
Die Schriftstellerin wird den neuen Roman *wohl* **geschrieben haben.**	The author has (probably) already written her new novel.

12. Verb Prefixes

German verbs have a number of prefixes that change their meaning, just as the prefixes "re-," "en-," and "ex-" change the English word "act" to produce "react," "enact," and "exact." There are two kinds of prefixes in German: separable and inseparable.

Separable Prefixes

1. Separable prefixes are usually removed from the present and preterite tense and placed at the end of the sentence or clause.

anfangen	to begin
Die Stunde fängt um 7.00 Uhr *an*.	The (class) hour begins at 7:00 o'clock.
aufmachen	to open
Der Lehrer machte das Buch *auf*.	The teacher opened the book.
zumachen	to close
Der Lehrer machte das Buch *zu*.	The teacher closed the book.

The most common separable prefixes in German have certain basic meanings that color the meaning of the verb to which they are attached.

ab-	away from, starting from, down from	*ein-*	into
an-	beginning	*her-*	from
auf-	upwards, opening	*hin-*	toward
aus-	out of	*nach-*	afterward, following upon
bei-	attending	*vor-*	in front of, beforehand
durch-	through	*zu-*	closing, adding to
		zurück-	back, returning

2. There are dozens of other separable verb prefixes. Historically many of these are formed from direct objects, such as

*teil***nehmen**	to participate (*lit.* "to take part")
*statt***finden**	to take place (*lit.* "to find place")
*stand***halten**	to stand firm

or adverbs, such as

*fern*sehen to watch television (*lit.* "to see far")
*fort*dauern to continue without interruption
*fest*halten to hold on (*lit.* "to hold firm")
*los*fahren to start off

or other verbs, such as

*stehen*bleiben to stop, to come to a stop (*lit.* "to remain standing")
*kennen*lernen to become acquainted with (*lit.* "to learn to know")

or old prepositional phrases, such as

*abhanden*kommen to become lost
*imstande*sein to be able to
*zurecht*kommen to fit in, to get along

3. By far the largest cohesive set of separable prefixes is formed with the two words *hin-* and *her-*. *Hin-* implies motion towards a point of interest; *her-* implies motion from a point of interest. Some representatives of the *hin-/her-* family are:

hinein-	go into	*herauf-*	come upstairs
herein-	come into	*hinauf-*	go upstairs
	Herein! = "Come in!"	*herunter-*	come downstairs
hinaus-	go out into	*hinunter-*	go downstairs
heraus-	come out into		

4. A number of verbs generate entire "families" of related verbs produced from the addition of separable (and inseparable) prefixes. Take, for example, *ziehen*, which has the basic meaning of "to pull" or "to draw (out)." Adding some of the prefixes listed earlier yields the following:

ziehen	to pull	*um*ziehen	to change clothing
*ab*ziehen	to run off a print	*zurück*ziehen	to move (pull) back
*an*ziehen	to dress, to put on clothing	*vor*ziehen	to prefer
*auf*ziehen	to wind up, to pull up		

Note: Many of the above prefixes look like prepositions. They are, however, part of their respective verbs. This can give rise to situations in which a prefix and its preposition look-alike can appear in the same sentence.

Er *stieg* aus dem Zug *aus*.   He got off (out of) the train.
Passen Sie *auf* die Stufe *auf*!   Watch out for the step!
Wir *fangen* am (= an dem) Montag *an*.   We are beginning on Monday.

Inseparable Prefixes

Inseparable prefixes are never removed from their verb forms. In fact, they even replace the *ge-* of the past participle. (See Chapter 10.) The inseparable prefixes also convey meaning, but the meanings are less tangible than those of separable prefixes.

- **be-** makes a verb transitive, that is, the verb takes an object
  kommen   to come
  *be*kommen   to get, obtain, receive (not "become")

  gehen   to go
  *be*gehen   to commit

- **emp-** (only three verbs have this prefix)
  fangen   to catch
  *emp*fangen   to receive

  fehlen   to be missing
  *emp*fehlen   to recommend

  finden   to find
  *emp*finden   to be sensitive to

- **ent-** away from, escape, removal
  nehmen   to take
  *ent*nehmen   to take from, to deduce

  laufen   to run
  *ent*laufen   to run away, to escape

  ziehen   to pull, to move
  *ent*ziehen   to move away from, to remove

- **er-** usually makes a verb transitive; frequently implies acquisition of some object by means of the verb
  kämpfen   to fight
  *er*kämpfen   to win something in a fight

  richten   to put something right
  *er*richten   to set up, to build, to erect

  zwingen   to force
  *er*zwingen   to get by force

- **ver-** reverses the verb action; frequently implies deviation from the verb action
  kaufen   to buy
  *ver*kaufen   to sell

  mieten   to rent from someone
  *ver*mieten   to lease to someone

  passen   to suit, to be suitable
  *ver*passen   to miss out on something

  sagen   to say
  *ver*sagen   to fail at something

zer-   an extreme verb action, implies "completely" or "to pieces"
    stören   to disturb
    zerstören   to destroy

    fallen   to fall
    zerfallen   to fall to pieces, to decay

    brechen   to break
    zerbrechen   to shatter

Separable and Inseparable Prefixes

A number of prefixes can be either separable or inseparable, although, when they are used with the same verb, the meaning of the verb is different in each case. The most common of these prefixes are *durch-*, *um-*, and *unter-*. Note that, when a prefix is separable, it is stressed in speech. When the prefix is inseparable, the verb (stem) is stressed.

*dúrch*reisen	(separable)	to travel through
*durch*réisen	(inseparable)	to traverse
*durch*súchen	(inseparable)	to search through, to frisk
*úm*schreiben	(separable)	to rewrite
*um*schréiben	(inseparable)	to paraphrase
*unter*bréchen	(inseparable)	to interrupt
*únter*gehen	(separable)	to go under, to decline
*unter*súchen	(inseparable)	to investigate

13. The Imperative

1. The imperative is used to issue commands and requests. In English, examples include:

    Open the door!   Let's go to the movies!
    Stand up!   Let's stay home this evening!
    Turn off the television!   Let's see the parade!

2. Since German has three forms corresponding to "you," there are three corresponding forms of the imperative. The *Sie*-imperative involves taking the present tense *Sie*-form of the verb and placing the *Sie* after the verb:

    Stehen Sie auf!   Stand/Get up!
    Kommen Sie her!   Come here!
    Trinken Sie den Kaffee!   Drink the coffee!
    Fahren Sie geradeaus!   Drive straight ahead!

3. The *ihr*-imperative is simpler yet. It is merely the present tense *ihr*-form of the verb in question without the *ihr*.

    Steht auf!   Stand up!
    Kommt her!   Come here!
    Trinkt nicht so viel Kaffee!   Don't drink so much coffee!
    Fahrt immer geradeaus weiter!   Keep on driving straight ahead!

4. The *du*-imperative is created by taking the *du*-form of the present tense and removing the *-st* ending.

    Steh auf!   Stand up!
    Komm her!   Come here!
    Gib mir die Zeitung!   Give me the newspaper!
    Schrei nicht so laut!   Don't yell so loud!
    Mach die Tür endlich zu!   Close the door once and for all!

Exception: Verbs that change their stem from *a* to *ä* in the present tense do *not* make this change in the *du*-imperative.

    Fahr weiter!   Drive on!
    Trag diese Tasche!   Carry this bag!
    Fall nicht vom Stuhl!   Don't fall off the chair!

5. The form of the imperative corresponding to English "Let's... is formed by taking the *wir*-form of the present tense and putting the pronoun *wir* after it:

Gehen wir jetzt nach Hause!	Let's go home now!
Schreiben wir an die Großmutter!	Let's write Grandmother!
Trinken wir ein Bier!	Let's drink a beer!

6. The imperative forms of *sein* are:

Seien Sie so lieb!	Be kind!
Seid freundlich!	Be friendly!
Sei gut!	Be good!
Seien wir ehrlich miteinander!	Let's be honest with each other!

7. There is a form of imperative that is used in street signs, warnings, recipes, and abrupt verbal exchanges. It involves an abbreviated sentence that omits the subject (*Sie, du, ihr*) and the modal verb (*nicht dürfen, müssen, sollen, nicht sollen*).

(Sie müssen) aufpassen.	(You have to) watch out.
Aufpassen!	Watch out!
Bitte nicht stören!	Please do not disturb!
Einfahrt freihalten!	Do not block the entrance!
Nicht ohne Batterie fahren!	Do not operate vehicle without the battery!
Vor Weihnachten nicht aufmachen!	Do not open before Christmas!
Eine Stunde bei 200 Grad backen!	Bake one hour at 200 degrees!

14. Present Tense of the Subjunctive

There are two sets of subjunctive tenses in German, the *hypothetical* and the *indirect discourse*.

The subjunctive mood is used to put distance between the speaker or writer and what he/she says or writes. It expresses wishes, statements contrary to fact, politeness, and indirectness. Examples of the subjunctive in English include:

I would like to go home now.
We would fly to the Bahamas, if we had the money!
They should have left yesterday.
If they had only left when we told them to!
He said he was going to come over later.

Hypothetical Subjunctive

1. The hypothetical subjunctive is by far the more common of the two sets of subjunctive tenses, and frequently serves the functions of both. The present tense hypothetical subjunctive is formed off the preterite stem of the indicative.* To this stem are added the following endings, if they are not already present.

ich	-e	wir	-en
du	-est	ihr	-et
man	-e	sie	-en

*Note: The term *indicative* refers to all the tense forms met up to now, with the exception of *imperative*. The terms *indicative*, *imperative*, and *subjunctive* are the three moods of German and English verbs.

2. In the case of most weak verbs the forms thus generated are exactly the same as the preterite indicative:

machen   to do, to make
(if) I did, (if) you did, etc.

ich machte	wir machten
du machtest	ihr machtet
man machte	sie machten

3. In the case of most strong verbs, the forms take an umlaut in their stem as well as the above endings:

sein to be
(if) I were, (if) you were, etc.

ich wäre	wir wären
du wärest	ihr wäret
man wäre	sie wären

Wenn ich ein Vöglein wär(e),	If I were a little bird,
Und auch zwei Flüglein hätt(e),	And had two little wings,
Flög(e) ich zu dir.	I would fly to you.
(Deutsches Volkslied)	(German folksong)

4. In practice, only a handful of verbs use their "pure" present subjunctive, in modern German. These include:

Infinitive	Present Subjunctive	
dürfen	dürfte	I might be permitted to
geben	gäbe	I would give
gehen	ginge	I would go
haben	hätte	I would have
kommen	käme	I would come
können	könnte	I might be able to, I could
lassen	liesse	I might permit, I might have (something) done
mögen	möchte	I would like to
sein	wäre	I would be
sollen*	sollte	I should, I ought to
werden	würde	I would
wissen	wüßte	I would know
wollen*	wollte	I would want to

*Note: *Sollen* and *wollen* do not take an umlaut in the subjunctive.

5. Most verbs use the appropriate present subjunctive of *werden* plus the infinitive just like the modal verb.

machen to do, to make
I would do, you would do, etc.

ich würde...machen	wir würden...machen
du würdest...machen	ihr würdet...machen
man würde...machen	sie würden...machen

As in the future tense with *werden*, the infinitive after *würde* will stand at the end of the sentence.

Wenn ich viel Geld hätte, würde ich ein großes Haus kaufen.	If I had a lot of money, I would buy a big house.
Wenn wir alle reich wären, würden wir auch unglücklich sein.	If we all were rich, we would also be unhappy.
Wenn ich besser schreiben könnte, würde ich viel schreiben.	If I could write better, I would write more.

6. This form of the subjunctive is also called the *general subjunctive, conditional, subjunctive II,* and even the *past subjunctive* (both present and past tense forms). The *würde*-subjunctive is also sometimes referred to as the *future subjunctive,* even though the hypothetical subjunctive cannot have either a present or a future, only a past and a "nonpast."

Indirect Discourse Subjunctive

1. The second form of the subjunctive is used almost exclusively to report statements made in writing or in spoken language by people other than the writer or speaker. English has a similar construction, using what looks like the past tense to render what someone said in the present.

> He said, "I am going home."
> He said that he *was going* home.
>
> She quoted him as saying, "I will not work here any more!"
> She quoted him as saying that he *would not work* here any more.
>
> I overheard them say, "We took the money and ran."
> I overheard them say that they *had taken* the money and *run.*

2. The indirect discourse subjunctive is sometimes also called *subjunctive I, special subjunctive,* and even the *present subjunctive.* Its forms represent the most regular tense in the German language, although its use is highly restricted. It uses the same endings as the hypothetical subjunctive.

ich	-e		wir	-en
du	-est		ihr	-et
man	-e		sie	-en

machen to do, to make
(He said that...) I do, you do, etc.

ich mache	wir machen
du machest	ihr machet
man mache	sie machen

However, the indirect discourse subjunctive does not use the preterite as a base. Instead, it uses the present tense stem without any changes (that is, stem-vowel changes such as those found in *geben, lesen, fahren, stossen* etc., do not apply).

sehen to see
(She said that...) I see, you see, etc.

ich sehe	wir sehen
du sehest	ihr sehet
man sehe	sie sehen

geben to give
(You said that...) I give, you give, etc.

ich gebe	wir geben
du gebest	ihr gebet
man gebe	sie geben

tragen to wear, to carry
(I said that...) I wear, you wear, etc.

ich trage	wir tragen
du tragest	ihr traget
man trage	sie tragen

Der Präsident sagte, daß er eine verbesserte Zukunft sehe. Es gebe immer noch 12% Arbeitslosigkeit. Das Volk trage aber diese Last mit Geduld.
(an example of extended indirect discourse)

The president said that he saw an improved future. There was still 12% unemployment. The people were, however, bearing this burden with patience.

3. The forms of the indirect discourse subjunctive are so regular that only *sein* has any irregularities, namely, no *-e* in the *ich* and *man* forms.

sein to be
(They said that...) I am, you are, etc.

ich sei	wir seien
du seiest	ihr seiet
man sei	sie seien

Der Minister sagte, daß er mit dem Vertrag einverstanden sei. Die Bedingungen seien alle in Ordnung. Die beiden Länder seien ausgezeichnete Handelspartner.
(an example of extended indirect discourse)

The minister said that he was satisfied with the treaty. The terms were all in order. The two countries were excellent trading partners.

The Future Tense of the Indirect Discourse Subjunctive

The indirect discourse subjunctive can have a future tense, unlike the hypothetical subjunctive. This is formed exactly like the future indicative or the subjunctive with *würde*, except that the indirect discourse subjunctive of *werden* is used:

machen to do, to make
(She said that...) I will do, you will do, etc.

ich werde...machen	wir werden...machen
du werdest...machen	ihr werdet...machen
man werde...machen	sie werden...machen

Der Minister sagte, daß er den Vertrag unterschreiben werde.

He said that he would sign the treaty.

Er meinte, daß der Vertrag die Zusammenarbeit erleichtern werde.

He was of the opinion that the treaty would make cooperation much easier.

15. Past Tense of the Subjunctive

The subjunctive can have a past tense, since there are situations where what might have occured did not in fact occur.

>If we hadn't taken the car, we would have been late.
>She would have been hurt, if she hadn't been an expert skier.

The subjunctive has only one past tense form, resembling the present perfect of the indicative. There is no preterite subjunctive. The past tense of the hypothetical subjunctive is created by using the appropriate form of *haben* or *sein* in the subjunctive plus the past participle.

>*machen*   to do, to make
>I would have done, you would have done, etc.

ich hätte (habe)...gemacht	wir hätten (haben)...gemacht
du hättest (habest)...gemacht	ihr hättet (habet)...gemacht
man hätte (habe)...gemacht	sie hätten (haben)...gemacht

>*gehen*   to go
>I would have gone, you would have gone, etc.

ich wäre (sei)...gegangen	wir wären (seien)...gegangen
du wärest (seiest)...gegangen	ihr wäret (seiet)...gegangen
man wäre (sei)...gegangen	sie wären (seien)...gegangen

Ich hätte das gemacht, wenn ich Zeit gehabt hätte.	I would have done that, if I had had time.
Wären wir doch alle zusammen ins Kino gegangen!	If only we had all gone together to the movies!
Er behauptet, er habe nichts gesehen.	He claims (that) he saw nothing.

Note: All modals take *haben* in the present perfect, whether indicative or subjunctive. The infinitive of the main verb is not relevant.

Wir hätten das nicht machen sollen.	We should not have done that.
Er hätte mitgehen können, wenn er das gewußt hätte.	He could have gone along, if he had known about it.

16. The Passive Voice

1. The passive voice is used to emphasize the activity performed, not the person performing the activity. In English, the passive is formed by using the appropriate form of "to be" plus the past participle.

> Bananas are grown in many tropical countries.
> Elk have been spotted again in those mountains.
> Letters are more easily typed than handwritten.

2. In German, the passive voice is created by using *werden* plus the past participle placed at the end of the clause.

sehen   to see
I am seen, you are seen, etc.

ich werde...gesehen	wir werden...gesehen
du wirst...gesehen	ihr werdet...gesehen
man wird...gesehen	sie werden...gesehen

Ich sehe und (ich) *werde gesehen*.	I see and am seen.
Ich höre und (ich) *werde gehört*.	I hear and am heard.
Ich rufe und (ich) *werde gerufen*.	I call and am called.
Bücher *werden* überall in der Bundesrepublik *gelesen*.	Books are read everywhere in the Federal Republic.
Ein Freund *wird* immer gern *eingeladen*.	A friend is always invited gladly.

3. The preterite passive uses the preterite of *werden*.

sehen   to see
I was seen, you were seen, etc.

ich wurde...gesehen	wir wurden...gesehen
du wurdest...gesehen	ihr wurdet...gesehen
man wurde...gesehen	sie wurden...gesehen

Ich sah and *wurde gesehen*.	I saw and was seen.
Ich hörte und *wurde gehört*.	I heard and was heard.
Bücher *wurden* schon im siebzehnten Jahrhundert in Deutschland *gedruckt*.	Books were already being printed in Germany in the seventeenth century.
Mein Freund Hans *wurde* von uns gestern *eingeladen*.	My friend Hans was invited by us yesterday.

4. The perfect passive tenses have patterns similar to their corresponding active (nonpassive) ones. But instead of *geworden* for the past participle of *werden,* an abbreviated form is used: *worden.* Remember that *werden* (*wurde, geworden/ worden*) requires the appropriate forms of *sein* in its compound tenses.

sehen to see
I have been seen, you have been seen, etc.

ich bin...gesehen worden	wir sind...gesehen worden
du bist...gesehen worden	ihr seid...gesehen worden
man ist...gesehen worden	sie sind...gesehen worden

Ich habe gesehen und *bin gesehen worden.*	I have seen and have been seen.
Bücher *sind* schon im 17. Jahrhundert in Deutschland *gedruckt worden.*	Books were printed in the 17th century in Germany.
Mein Freund *ist* von uns *eingeladen worden.*	My friend was/has been invited by us.

5. The future passive simply requires the future forms of *werden.*

sehen to see
I will be seen, you will be seen, etc.

ich werde...gesehen werden	wir werden...gesehen werden
du wirst...gesehen werden	ihr werdet...gesehen werden
man wird...gesehen werden	sie werden...gesehen werden

Ich werde sehen und *werde gesehen werden.*	I will see and will be seen.
Bücher *werden* hoffentlich auch im 21. Jahrhundert *gedruckt werden.*	Books will hopefully be printed in the 21st century, too.

6. Other passive tenses follow patterns similar to those for the active tenses.

Past Perfect:

Ich hatte gesehen und *war gesehen worden.*	I had seen and had been seen.

Future Perfect:

Ich werde gesehen haben und *werde gesehen worden sein.*	I will have seen and will have been seen.

Present Subjunctive:

Ich würde sehen und *würde gesehen werden.*	I would see and would be seen.

Past Subjunctive:

Ich hätte gesehen und *wäre gesehen worden.*	I would have seen and would have been seen.

7. When the agent (doer) must be expressed in German, the preposition *von* ("by") is used.

Ich sehe ihn.	I see him.
Er wird *von mir* gesehen.	He is seen *by me*.
Er sieht mich.	He sees me.
Ich werde *von ihm* gesehen.	I am seen *by him*.

17. Summary of Verb Forms

Major Patterns

All inflected verbs, that is, verbs with endings, have at least the following endings, depending on the person and number of the subject of the verb to which they are attached.

ich	-		wir	-n
du	-st		ihr	-t
man	—		sie	-n

The following verbs represent all major inflectional patterns of German verbs: *empfehlen, haben, kommen, können, sein, suchen, werden.*

Although all the forms of *haben, sein,* and *werden* have already been presented, they are brought together here for easier reference. *Machen* has been used to illustrate the basic patterns of weak verbs; *suchen* will be used to give the reader another verb to look at. *Können* represents the modals. *Empfehlen* represents verbs with a stem-vowel change in the present tense as well as a verb with an inseparable prefix. *Kommen* represents verbs conjugated with *sein* in the perfect tenses.

The order of presentation of the tenses follows that used in this book.

empfehlen to recommend

Present: *I recommend, etc.*

ich empfehle wir empfehlen
du empfiehlst ihr empfehlt
man empfiehlt sie empfehlen

Future: *I will recommend, etc.*

ich werde...empfehlen wir werden...empfehlen
du wirst...empfehlen ihr werdet...empfehlen
man wird...empfehlen sie werden...empfehlen

Preterite: *I recommended, etc.*

ich empfahl wir empfahlen
du empfahlst ihr empfahlt
man empfahl sie empfahlen

Present Perfect: *I recommended, I have recommended, etc.*

ich habe...empfohlen wir haben...empfohlen
du hast...empfohlen ihr habt...empfohlen
man hat...empfohlen sie haben...empfohlen

Past Perfect: *I had recommended, etc.*

ich hatte...empfohlen	wir hatten...empfohlen
du hattest...empfohlen	ihr hattet...empfohlen
man hatte...empfohlen	sie hatten...empfohlen

Future perfect: *I will have recommended, etc.*

ich werde...empfohlen haben	wir werden...empfohlen haben
du wirst...empfohlen haben	ihr werdet...empfohlen haben
man wird...empfohlen haben	sie werden...empfohlen haben

Imperative: *Recommend! Let's recommend!*

(du)	empfiehl!	recommend!
(wir)	empfehlen wir!	let's recommend!
(ihr)	empfehlt!	
(Sie)	empfehlen Sie!	

Present Subjunctive without *würde*: *I would recommend, etc.*

ich empfähle	wir empfählen
du empfählest	ihr empfählet
man empfähle	sie empfählen

Present Subjunctive with *würde*: *I would recommend, etc.*

ich würde...empfehlen	wir würden...empfehlen
du würdest...empfehlen	ihr würdet...empfehlen
man würde...empfehlen	sie würden...empfehlen

Present Subjunctive (indirect discourse): *(He said that...) I recommend, etc.*

ich empfehle	wir empfehlen
du empfehlest	ihr empfehlet
man empfehle	sie empfehlen

Future Subjunctive (indirect discourse): *(They said that...) I will recommend, etc.*

ich werde...empfehlen	wir werden...empfehlen
du werdest...empfehlen	ihr werdet...empfehlen
man werde...empfehlen	sie werden...empfehlen

Past Subjunctive *I would have recommended, etc.*

ich hätte...empfohlen	wir hätten...empfohlen
du hättest...empfohlen	ihr hättet...empfohlen
man hätte...empfohlen	sie hätten...empfohlen

Past Subjunctive (indirect discourse): *(She said that...) I had recommended, etc.*

ich habe...empfohlen	wir haben...empfohlen
du habest...empfohlen	ihr habet...empfohlen
man habe...empfohlen	sie haben...empfohlen

Present Passive: *I am (being) recommended, etc.*

ich werde...empfohlen	wir werden...empfohlen
du wirst...empfohlen	ihr werdet...empfohlen
man wird...empfohlen	sie werden...empfohlen

Preterite Passive: *I was (being) recommended, etc.*

ich wurde...empfohlen	wir wurden...empfohlen
du wurdest...empfohlen	ihr wurdet...empfohlen
man wurde...empfohlen	sie wurden...empfohlen

Present Perfect Passive: *I was (being) recommended, I have been recommended, etc.*

ich bin...empfohlen worden	wir sind...empfohlen worden
du bist...empfohlen worden	ihr seid...empfohlen worden
man ist...empfohlen worden	sie sind...empfohlen worden

Past Perfect Passive: *I had been recommended, etc.*

ich war...empfohlen worden	wir waren...empfohlen worden
du warst...empfohlen worden	ihr wart...empfohlen worden
man war...empfohlen worden	sie waren...empfohlen worden

Future Passive: *I will be recommended, etc.*

ich werde...empfohlen werden	wir werden...empfohlen werden
du wirst...empfohlen werden	ihr werdet...empfohlen werden
man wird...empfohlen werden	sie werden...empfohlen werden

haben to have

Present: *I have, etc.*

ich habe	wir haben
du hast	ihr habt
man hat	sie haben

Future: *I will have, etc.*

ich werde...haben	wir werden...haben
du wirst...haben	ihr werdet...haben
man wird...haben	sie werden...haben

Preterite: *I had, etc.*

ich hatte	wir hatten
du hattest	ihr hattet
man hatte	sie hatten

Present Perfect: *I had, I have had, etc.*

ich habe...gehabt	wir haben...gehabt
du hast...gehabt	ihr habt...gehabt
man hat...gehabt	sie haben...gehabt

Past Perfect: *I had had, etc.*

ich hatte...gehabt
du hattest...gehabt
man hatte...gehabt

wir hatten...gehabt
ihr hattet...gehabt
sie hatten...gehabt

Future Perfect: *I will have had, etc.*

ich werde...gehabt haben
du wirst...gehabt haben
man wird...gehabt haben

wir werden...gehabt haben
ihr werdet...gehabt haben
sie werden...gehabt haben

Imperative: *Have! Let's have!*

(du)   hab(e)!
(wir) haben wir!
(ihr) habt!
(Sie) haben Sie!

Present Subjunctive without *würde*: *I would have, etc.*

ich hätte
du hättest
man hätte

wir hätten
ihr hättet
sie hätten

Present Subjunctive with *würde**

*Note: These forms are normally not used. Hereafter, forms that are not used will not be listed.

Present Subjunctive (indirect discourse): *(I said that...) I have, etc.*

ich habe
du habest
man habe

wir haben
ihr habet
sie haben

Future Subjunctive (indirect discourse): *(You said that...) I will have, etc.*

ich werde...haben
du werdest...haben
man werde...haben

wir werden...haben
ihr werdet...haben
sie werden...haben

Past Subjunctive: *I would have had, etc.*

ich hätte...gehabt
du hättest...gehabt
man hätte...gehabt

wir hätten...gehabt
ihr hättet...gehabt
sie hätten...gehabt

Past Subjunctive (indirect discourse): *(We said that...) I had, etc.*

ich habe...gehabt
du habest...gehabt
man habe...gehabt

wir haben...gehabt
ihr habet...gehabt
sie haben...gehabt

Present Passive**

ich werde...gehabt
du wirst...gehabt
man wird...gehabt

wir werden...gehabt
ihr werdet...gehabt
sie werden...gehabt

Preterite Passive**

ich wurde...gehabt	wir wurden...gehabt
du wurdest...gehabt	ihr wurdet...gehabt
man wurde...gehabt	sie wurden...gehabt

Present Perfect Passive**

ich bin...gehabt worden	wir sind...gehabt worden
du bist...gehabt worden	ihr seid...gehabt worden
man ist...gehabt worden	sie sind...gehabt worden

Past Perfect Passive**

ich war...gehabt worden	wir waren...gehabt worden
du warst...gehabt worden	ihr wart...gehabt worden
man war...gehabt worden	sie waren...gehabt worden

Future Passive**

ich werde...gehabt werden	wir werden...gehabt werden
du wirst...gehabt werden	ihr werdet...gehabt werden
man wird...gehabt werden	sie werden...gehabt werden

**Note: *Haben* is rarely used in the passive voice, although there are verbs with prefixes that do have passive forms, such as *vorhaben* (separable) "to intend," "to plan;" *handhaben* "to operate," "to manipulate." The passive forms of *haben* are listed here for reference only. English "have" in the sense of "I had cereal for breakfast" or "We have been had by the government" cannot normally be translated as *haben* in German.

kommen   to come

Present: *I come, I am coming, etc.*

ich komme	wir kommen
du kommst	ihr kommt
man kommt	sie kommen

Future: *I will come, etc.*

ich werde...kommen	wir werden...kommen
du wirst...kommen	ihr werdet...kommen
man wird...kommen	sie werden...kommen

Preterite: *I came, etc.*

ich kam	wir kamen
du kamst	ihr kamt
man kam	sie kamen

Present Perfect: *I came, I have come, etc.*

ich bin...gekommen	wir sind...gekommen
du bist...gekommen	ihr seid...gekommen
man ist...gekommen	sie sind...gekommen

Past Perfect: *I had come, etc.*

ich war...gekommen   wir waren...gekommen
du warst...gekommen   ihr wart...gekommen
man war...gekommen   sie waren...gekommen

Future Perfect: *I will have come, etc.*

ich werde...gekommen sein   wir werden...gekommen sein
du wirst...gekommen sein   ihr werdet...gekommen sein
man wird...gekommen sein   sie werden...gekommen sein

Imperative: *Come! Let's come!*

(du)   komm!
(wir) kommen wir!
(ihr) kommt!
(Sie) kommen Sie!

Present Subjunctive without *würde*: *I would come, etc.*

ich käme   wir kämen
du kämest   ihr kämet
man käme   sie kämen

Present Subjunctive with *würde*: *I would come, etc.*

ich würde...kommen   wir würden...kommen
du würdest...kommen   ihr würdet...kommen
man würde...kommen   sie würden...kommen

Present Subjunctive (indirect discourse): *(I said that... I come, etc.)*

ich komme   wir kommen
du kommest   ihr kommet
man komme   sie kommen

Future Subjunctive (indirect discourse): *(She said that...) I will come, etc.*

ich werde...kommen   wir werden...kommen
du werdest...kommen   ihr werdet...kommen
man werde...kommen   sie werden...kommen

Past Subjunctive: *I would have come, etc.*

ich wäre...gekommen   wir wären...gekommen
du wärest...gekommen   ihr wäret...gekommen
man wäre...gekommen   sie wären...gekommen

Past Subjunctive (indirect discourse): *(They said that...) I have come, etc.*

ich sei...gekommen   wir seien...gekommen
du seiest...gekommen   ihr seiet...gekommen
man sei...gekommen   sie seien...gekommen

können to be able to
Present: *I can, I am able to, etc.*

ich kann	wir können
du kannst	ihr könnt
man kann	sie können

Future: *I will be able to, etc.*

ich werde...können	wir werden...können
du wirst...können	ihr werdet...können
man wird...können	sie werden...können

Preterite: *I was able to, I could, etc.*

ich konnte	wir konnten
du konntest	ihr konntet
man konnte	sie konnten

Present Perfect: *I was able to, I have been able to, etc.*

ich habe...können (gekonnt)	wir haben...können (gekonnt)
du hast...können (gekonnt)	ihr habt...können (gekonnt)
man hat...können (gekonnt)	sie haben...können (gekonnt)

Past Perfect: *I had been able to, etc.*

ich hatte ...können (gekonnt)	wir hatten...können (gekonnt)
du hattest...können (gekonnt)	ihr hattet...können (gekonnt)
man hatte...können (gekonnt)	sie hatten...können (gekonnt)

Present Subjunctive without *würde*: *I would be able to, I could, etc.*

ich könnte	wir könnten
du könntest	ihr könntet
man könnte	sie könnten

Present Subjunctive (indirect discourse): *(I said that...) I would be able to, etc.*

ich könne	wir können
du könnest	ihr könnet
man könne	sie können

Future Subjunctive (indirect discourse): *(He said that...) I will be able to, etc.*

ich werde...können	wir werden...können
du werdest...können	ihr werdet...können
man werde...können	sie werden...können

Past Subjunctive: *I would have been able to, etc.*

ich hätte...können (gekonnt)	wir hätten...können (gekonnt)
du hättest...können (gekonnt)	ihr hättet...können (gekonnt)
man hätte...können (gekonnt)	sie hätten...können (gekonnt)

Past Subjunctive (indirect discourse:) *(We said that...) I was able to, etc.*

ich habe...können (gekonnt)	wir haben...können (gekonnt)
du habest...können (gekonnt)	ihr habet...können (gekonnt)
man habe...können (gekonnt)	sie haben...können (gekonnt)

sein to be

Present: *I am, etc.*

ich bin	wir sind
du bist	ihr seid
man ist	sie sind

Future: *I will be, etc.*

ich werde...sein	wir werden...sein
du wirst...sein	ihr werdet...sein
man wird...sein	sie werden...sein

Preterite: *I was, etc.*

ich war	wir waren
du warst	ihr wart
man war	sie waren

Present Perfect: *I was, I have been, etc.*

ich bin...gewesen	wir sind...gewesen
du bist...gewesen	ihr seid...gewesen
man ist...gewesen	sie sind...gewesen

Past Perfect: *I had been, etc.*

ich war...gewesen	wir waren...gewesen
du warst...gewesen	ihr wart...gewesen
man war...gewesen	sie waren...gewesen

Future Perfect: *I will have been, etc.*

ich werde...gewesen sein	wir werden...gewesen sein
du wirst...gewesen sein	ihr werdet...gewesen sein
man wird...gewesen sein	sie werden...gewesen sein

Imperative: *Be!, Let's be!*

(du)	sei!
(wir)	seien wir!
(ihr)	seid!
(Sie)	seien Sie!

Present Subjunctive without *würde*: *I would be, etc.*

ich wäre	wir wären
du wärest	ihr wäret
man wäre	sie wären

Present Subjunctive (indirect discourse): *(She said that...) I am, etc.*

ich sei	wir seien
du seiest	ihr seiet
man sei	sie seien

Future Subjunctive (indirect discourse): *(They said that...) I will be, etc.*

ich werde...sein	wir werden...sein
du werdest...sein	ihr werdet...sein
man werde...sein	sie werden...sein

Past Subjunctive: *I would have been, etc.*

ich wäre...gewesen	wir wären...gewesen
du wärest...gewesen	ihr wäret...gewesen
man wäre...gewesen	sie wären...gewesen

Past Subjunctive (indirect discourse): *(He said that...) I was, etc.*

ich sei...gewesen	wir seien...gewesen
du seiest...gewesen	ihr seiet...gewesen
man sei...gewesen	sie seien...gewesen

suchen   to look for

Present: *I look for, etc.*

ich suche	wir suchen
du suchst	ihr sucht
man sucht	sie suchen

Future: *I will look for, etc.*

ich werde...suchen	wir werden...suchen
du wirst...suchen	ihr werdet...suchen
man wird...suchen	sie werden...suchen

Preterite: *I looked for, etc.*

ich suchte	wir suchten
du suchtest	ihr suchtet
man suchte	sie suchten

Present Perfect: *I looked for, I have looked for, etc.*

ich habe...gesucht	wir haben...gesucht
du hast...gesucht	ihr habt...gesucht
man hat...gesucht	sie haben...gesucht

Past Perfect: *I had looked for, etc.*

ich hatte...gesucht	wir hatten...gesucht
du hattest...gesucht	ihr hattet...gesucht
man hatte...gesucht	sie hatten...gesucht

Future Perfect: *I will have looked for, etc.*

ich werde...gesucht haben
du wirst...gesucht haben
man wird...gesucht haben

wir werden...gesucht haben
ihr werdet...gesucht haben
sie werden...gesucht haben

Imperative: *Look for!, Let's look for!*

(du) such(e)!
(wir) suchen wir!
(ihr) sucht!
(Sie) suchen Sie!

Present Subjunctive without *würde*: *I would look for, etc.*

ich suchte
du suchtest
man suchte

wir suchten
ihr suchtet
sie suchten

Present Subjunctive with *würde*: *I would look for, etc.*

ich würde...suchen
du würdest...suchen
man würde...suchen

wir würden...suchen
ihr würdet...suchen
sie würden...suchen

Present Subjunctive (indirect discourse): *(You said that...) I look for, etc.*

ich suche
du suchest
man suche

wir suchen
ihr suchet
sie suchen

Future Subjunctive (indirect discourse): *(We said that...) I will look for, etc.*

ich werde...suchen
du werdest...suchen
man werde...suchen

wir werden...suchen
ihr werdet...suchen
sie werden...suchen

Past Subjunctive: *I would have looked for, etc.*

ich hätte...gesucht
du hättest...gesucht
man hätte...gesucht

wir hätten...gesucht
ihr hättet...gesucht
sie hätten...gesucht

Past Subjunctive (indirect discourse): *(They said that...) I looked for, etc.*

ich habe...gesucht
du habest...gesucht
man habe...gesucht

wir haben...gesucht
ihr habet...gesucht
sie haben...gesucht

Present Passive: *I am (being) looked for, etc.*

ich werde...gesucht
du wirst...gesucht
man wird...gesucht

wir werden...gesucht
ihr werdet...gesucht
sie werden...gesucht

Preterite Passive: *I was (being) looked for, etc.*

ich wurde...gesucht
du wurdest...gesucht
man wurde...gesucht

wir wurden...gesucht
ihr wurdet...gesucht
sie wurden...gesucht

Present Perfect Passive: *I was (being) looked for, I have been looked for, etc.*

ich bin...gesucht worden
du bist...gesucht worden
man ist...gesucht worden

wir sind...gesucht worden
ihr seid...gesucht worden
sie sind...gesucht worden

Past Perfect Passive: *I had been looked for, etc.*

ich war...gesucht worden
du warst...gesucht worden
man war...gesucht worden

wir waren...gesucht worden
ihr wart...gesucht worden
sie waren...gesucht worden

Future Passive: *I will have been looked for, etc.*

ich werde...gesucht werden
du wirst...gesucht werden
man wird...gesucht werden

wir werden...gesucht werden
ihr werdet...gesucht werden
sie werden...gesucht werden

werden to become

Present: *I become, etc.*

ich werde
du wirst
man wird

wir werden
ihr werdet
sie werden

Future: *I will become, etc.*

ich werde...werden
du wirst...werden
man wird...werden

wir werden...werden
ihr werdet...werden
sie werden...werden

Preterite: *I became, etc.*

ich würde
du würdest
man würde

wir würden
ihr würdet
sie würden

Present Perfect: *I became, I have become, etc.*

ich bin...geworden
du bist...geworden
man ist...geworden

wir sind...geworden
ihr seid...geworden
sie sind...geworden

Past Perfect: *I had become, etc.*

ich war...geworden
du warst...geworden
man war...geworden

wir waren...geworden
ihr wart...geworden
sie waren...geworden

Future Perfect: *I will have become, etc.*

ich werde...geworden sein	wir werden...geworden sein
du wirst...geworden sein	ihr werdet...geworden sein
man wird...geworden sein	sie werden...geworden sein

Present Subjunctive without *würde: I would become, etc.*

ich würde	wir würden
du würdest	ihr würdet
man würde	sie würden

Present Subjunctive with *würde: I would become, etc.*

ich würde...werden	wir würden...werden
du würdest...werden	ihr würdet...werden
man würde...werden	sie würden...werden

Present Subjunctive (indirect discourse): *(He said that...) I become, etc.*

ich werde	wir werden
du werdest	ihr werdet
man werde	sie werden

Future Subjunctive (indirect discourse): *(We said that...) I will become, etc.*

ich werde...werden	wir werden...werden
du werdest...werden	ihr werdet...werden
man werde...werden	sie werden...werden

Past Subjunctive: *I would have become, etc.*

ich wäre...geworden	wir wären...geworden
du wärest...geworden	ihr wäret...geworden
man wäre...geworden	sie wären...geworden

Past Subjunctive (indirect discourse): *(I said that...) I became, etc.*

ich sei...geworden	wir seien...geworden
du seiest...geworden	ihr seiet...geworden
man sei...geworden	sie seien...geworden

Principal Parts

Strong Verbs

The following is a list of the most common strong verbs and their principal parts. (*S* indicates a verb that takes *sein* in its compound tenses. * indicates a verb with a prefix that takes *haben*, even though its base verb takes *sein*. For example, *Er ist gefahren*, but *Er hat erfahren*.)

Infinitive	Preterite	Past Participle	
beginnen	begann	begonnen	to begin
bieten	bot	geboten	to offer
anbieten	bot...an	angeboten	to make an offer
verbieten	verbot	verboten	to forbid
binden	band	gebunden	to tie, to bind
bitten	bat	gebeten	to ask (a favor)
bleiben	blieb	geblieben (S)	to stay, to remain
brechen (bricht)	brach	gebrochen	to break
zerbrechen (zerbricht)	zerbrach	zerbrochen	to shatter
bringen	brachte	gebracht	to bring
verbringen	verbrachte	verbracht	to spend (time)
denken	dachte	gedacht	to think
dürfen (darf)	durfte	dürfen (gedurft)	to be allowed to
empfehlen (empfiehlt)	empfahl	empfohlen	to recommend
essen (ißt)	aß	gegessen	to eat
fahren (fährt)	fuhr	gefahren (S)	to go by vehicle
erfahren (erfährt)	erfuhr	erfahren*	to learn about something
fallen (fällt)	fiel	gefallen (S)	to fall
gefallen (gefällt)	gefiel	gefallen*	to please
fangen (fängt)	fing	gefangen	to catch
anfangen (fängt ...an)	fing ...an	angefangen	to begin
finden	fand	gefunden	to find
erfinden	erfand	erfunden	to invent
geben (gibt)	gab	gegeben	to give
aufgeben (gibt ...auf)	gab ...auf	aufgegeben	to give up
ausgeben (gibt ...aus)	gab ...aus	ausgegeben	to spend (money)
umgeben (umgibt)	umgab	umgeben	to surround
gehen	ging	gegangen (S)	to go
begehen	beging	begangen*	to commit (a crime)
geniessen	genoß	genossen	to enjoy
greifen	griff	gegriffen	to grasp
begreifen	begriff	begriffen	to comprehend
haben (hat)	hatte	gehabt	to have
vorhaben (hat...vor)	hatte...vor	vorgehabt	to intend
halten (hält)	hielt	gehalten	to hold, to stop
behalten (behält)	behielt	behalten	to keep
erhalten (erhält)	erhielt	erhalten	to receive
hängen	hing	gehangen	to hang
heben	hob	gehoben	to lift
heißen	hieß	geheissen	to be named
helfen (hilft)	half	geholfen	to help

Infinitive	Preterite	Past Participle	
kennen	kannte	gekannt	to know (a person)
erkennen	erkannte	erkannt	to recognize
kommen	kam	gekommen (S)	to come
bekommen	bekam	bekommen*	to get, to obtain
können (kann)	konnte	können (gekonnt)	to be able to
laden (lädt)	lud	geladen	to load
einladen (lädt ...ein)	lud ...ein	eingeladen	to invite
lassen (lässt)	ließ	gelassen	to have (something done)
verlassen (verlässt)	verließ	verlassen	to abandon
laufen (läuft)	lief	gelaufen (S)	to run
leiden	litt	gelitten	to suffer
lesen (liest)	las	gelesen	to read
liegen	lag	gelegen	to lie, to be in a horizontal position
lügen	log	gelogen	to tell a lie
mögen (mag)	mochte	mögen (gemocht)	to like
müssen (muß)	mußte	müssen (gemusst)	to have to
nehmen (nimmt)	nahm	genommen	to take
nennen	nannte	genannt	to name
raten (rät)	riet	geraten	to give advice
beraten (berät)	beriet	beraten	to advise (someone)
zerreißen	riß	gerissen	to tear
reißen	zerriß	zerrissen	to tear to shreds
rennen	rannte	gerannt (S)	to run
riechen	roch	gerochen	to smell
rufen	rief	gerufen	to call
anrufen	rief ...an	angerufen	to call on the telephone
schlafen (schläft)	schlief	geschlafen	to sleep
schlagen (schlägt)	schlug	geschlagen	to hit
vorschlagen (schlägt ...vor)	schlug ...vor	vorgeschlagen	to suggest
schiessen	schoß	geschossen	to shoot
schließen	schloß	geschlossen	to close
schmelzen (schmilzt)	schmolz	geschmolzen	to melt
schneiden	schnitt	geschnitten	to cut
schreiben	schrieb	geschrieben	to write
beschreiben	beschrieb	beschrieben	to describe
verschreiben	verschrieb	verschrieben	to prescribe
vorschreiben	schrieb ...vor	vorgeschrieben	to require
schreien	schrie	geschrien	to cry, to yell
schwimmen	schwamm	geschwommen	to swim
sehen (sieht)	sah	gesehen	to see
einsehen (sieht...ein)	sah ...ein	eingesehen	to understand, to have insight

Infinitive	Preterite	Past Participle	
sein	war	gewesen (S)	to be
singen	sang	gesungen	to sing
sinken	sank	gesunken (S)	to sink
sitzen	saß	gesessen	to sit
besitzen	besaß	besessen	to own
sollen (soll)	sollte	sollen (gesollt)	to be obligated to
sprechen (spricht)	sprach	gesprochen	to speak
aussprechen (spricht ...aus)	sprach ...aus	ausgesprochen	to pronounce
besprechen (bespricht)	besprach	besprochen	to discuss
versprechen (verspricht)	versprach	versprochen	to promise
springen	sprang	gesprungen (S)	to jump
stehen	stand	gestanden	to stand
aufstehen	stand ...auf	aufgestanden (S)	to get up
verstehen	verstand	verstanden	to understand
steigen	stieg	gestiegen (S)	to climb
aussteigen	stieg ...aus	ausgestiegen (S)	to get out
einsteigen	stieg ...ein	eingestiegen (S)	to get in
umsteigen	stieg ...um	umgestiegen (S)	to change (planes)
besteigen	bestieg	bestiegen*	to climb a mountain
sterben (stirbt)	starb	gestorben (S)	to die
stinken	stank	gestunken	to stink
tragen (trägt)	trug	getragen	to carry, to wear clothes
trinken	trank	getrunken	to drink
ertrinken	ertrank	ertrunken (S)	to drown
vergessen (vergisst)	vergaß	vergessen	to forget
verlieren	verlor	verloren	to lose
wachsen (wächst)	wuchs	gewachsen (S)	to grow up
waschen (wäscht)	wusch	gewaschen	to wash
werden (wird)	wurde	geworden (S)	to become
werfen (wirft)	warf	geworfen	to throw
wiegen	wog	gewogen	to weigh
wissen (weiß)	wußte	gewußt	to know (a fact)
wollen (will)	wollte	wollen (gewollt)	to want to
ziehen	zog	gezogen	to pull
anziehen	zog ...an	angezogen	to put on (clothes)
ausziehen	zog ...aus	ausgezogen	to take off (clothes)
ausziehen	zog ...aus	ausgezogen (S)	to move out
einziehen	zog ...ein	eingezogen (S)	to move in
umziehen	zog ...um	umgezogen	to change (clothes)
umziehen	zog ...um	umgezogen (S)	to move (from one place to another)
zwingen	zwang	gezwungen	to force

Weak Verbs

The following is a list of the most common weak verbs that have prefixes. All other weak verbs follow the regular pattern. (*S* in this list indicates a verb that takes *sein* in its compound tenses.)

Infinitive	Preterite	Past Participle	
antworten	antwortete	geantwortet	to give an answer
beantworten	beantwortete	beantwortet	to answer a question
brauchen	brauchte	gebraucht	to need
gebrauchen	gebrauchte	gebraucht	to use
verbrauchen	verbrauchte	verbraucht	to consume, to use up
decken	deckte	gedeckt	to cover
entdecken	entdeckte	entdeckt	to discover
drucken	druckte	gedruckt	to print
drücken	drückte	gedrückt	to press, to push
ausdrücken	drückte ...aus	ausgedrückt	to express
fordern	forderte	gefordert	to demand
fördern	förderte	gefördert	to support, to further
befördern	beförderte	befördert	to promote someone
führen	führte	geführt	to lead
entführen	entführte	entführt	to abduct
verführen	verführte	verführt	to seduce
holen	holte	geholt	to fetch, to get
abholen	holte ...ab	abgeholt	to pick up
hören	hörte	gehört	to hear, to listen
aufhören	hörte ...auf	aufgehört	to cease, to stop
gehören	gehörte	gehört	to belong to
kaufen	kaufte	gekauft	to buy
verkaufen	verkaufte	verkauft	to sell
leben	lebte	gelebt	to be alive, to live
erleben	erlebte	erlebt	to experience
mieten	mietete	gemietet	to rent
vermieten	vermietete	vermietet	to rent out
sagen	sagte	gesagt	to say, to tell
versagen	versagte	versagt	to fail at something
schalten	schaltete	geschaltet	to operate a switch
abschalten	schaltete ...ab	abgeschaltet	to shut down
ausschalten	schaltete ...aus	ausgeschaltet	to turn off
einschalten	schaltete ...ein	eingeschaltet	to turn on
umschalten	schaltete ...um	umgeschaltet	to switch over
setzen	setzte	gesetzt	to set
besetzen	besetzte	besetzt	to occupy
versetzen	versetzte	versetzt	to transfer (someone)

Infinitive	Preterite	Past Participle	
steigern	steigerte	gesteigerte	to increase
ersteigern	ersteigerte	ersteigert	to win at an auction
versteigern	versteigerte	versteigert	to auction off
stellen	stellte	gestellt	to place upright
bestellen	bestellte	bestellt	to place an order
stören	störte	gestört	to disturb
zerstören	zerstörte	zerstört	to destroy
suchen	suchte	gesucht	to look for
besuchen	besuchte	besucht	to visit
versuchen	versuchte	versucht	to try
teilen	teilte	geteilt	to divide, to share
verteilen	verteilte	verteilt	to distribute
wandern	wanderte	gewandert (S)	to hike
auswandern	wanderte ...aus	ausgewandert (S)	to emigrate
einwandern	wanderte ...ein	eingewandert (S)	to immigrate
warten	wartete	gewartet	to wait
erwarten	erwartete	erwartet	to expect
zahlen	zahlte	gezahlt	to pay
bezahlen	bezahlen	bezahlt	to pay a bill
zählen	zählte	gezählt	to count
erzählen	erzählte	erzählt	to tell a story
zeichnen	zeichnete	gezeichnet	to draw a picture
bezeichnen	bezeichnete	bezeichnet	to characterize

Part Two:
Essentials of Grammar

18. The Article

Nouns and pronouns in German have markers that indicate gender, number, and case. In English only certain pronouns have clear gender, number, and case markings, including "he," "she," "him," "her," and "it." Most English nouns are marked for number, but not for case or gender.

Singular	*Plural*
the book	the books
the boy	the boys
the goose	the geese
the lady	the ladies
the man	the men

German, however, has a complete set of markers for gender, number, and case. These are clearly present on the pronoun, but not always on the noun itself. The definite article, equivalent to English "the," which always precedes the noun, has the endings to distinguish gender, number, and case.

	Masculine	Singular Feminine	Neuter	Plural
Nominative	der	die	das	die
Accusative	den	die	das	die
Dative	dem	der	dem	den
Genitive	des	der	des	der

The indefinite article (English "a/an") has the following forms:

	Masculine	Feminine	Neuter
Nominative	ein	eine	ein
Accusative	einen	eine	ein
Dative	einem	einer	einem
Genitive	eines	einer	eines

Gender, number, and case are discussed in detail in Chapter 19, **Nouns**.

19. Nouns

Gender

1. The gender of German nouns is identified by the endings attached to articles and other demonstratives. Grammatical gender in German often has little to do with natural gender (sex). Thus, a noun is replaced by its appropriate pronoun.

Singular

der Tisch*	the table	er	it
die Tasche	the pocket	sie	it
das Tuch	the cloth	es	it

*Note: German nouns are *always* capitalized, no matter what their position in a sentence.

Plural

die Tische	the tables	sie	they
die Taschen	the pockets	sie	they
die Tücher	the cloths	sie	they

The subject pronouns introduced in Chapter 2 illustrate the relation between gender of nouns and gender of pronouns. Note that in the plural no distinction is made as to gender.

2. The gender of German nouns cannot always be determined by its written or spoken form. To English speakers, the gender of German nouns often seems very arbitrary. There are, however, a number of rules that apply to large categories of nouns.

The names of male beings are generally masculine (*der*).

der Mann	man, husband	der Bär	bear
der Hahn	rooster	der Lehrer	teacher (male)
der Hengst	stallion		

The names of female beings are generally feminine (*die*).

die Frau	woman	die Bärin	she-bear
die Henne	hen	die Lehrerin	teacher (female)
die Stute	mare		

All nouns that end in *-chen* or *-lein* are neuter (*das*). There are no exceptions to this rule.

| das Männlein | little man | das Fingerchen | small finger |
| das Fräulein | Miss | das Tischlein | little table |

All nouns that end in *-ung, -heit/-keit, -tät, -ei, -erei, -ie,* and *-schaft* are feminine *(die)*. There are no exceptions to this rule.

die Übung exercise	die Melodie melody
die Schönheit beauty	die Freundschaft friendship
die Einigkeit unity	die Bäckerei bakery
die Universität university	

The names of the letters of the alphabet are neuter *(das)*.

das F in "fein" the F in "fine"	das ABC the ABCs

The names of cities are neuter *(das)*, although the article is not ordinarily used with place names.

(das) Berlin	*(das)* Paris
(das) London	*(das)* New York

The names of *most* countries are neuter *(das)*. (Articles are *not* ordinarily used with the names of countries of neuter gender.)

(das) Deutschland Germany	*(das)* Norwegen Norway
(das) Amerika America	*(das)* Dänemark Denmark
(das) Italien Italy	

The names of the following countries are feminine *(die)*. (Articles *must* accompany the names of countries of feminine gender.)

die Schweiz Switzerland	die Vatikanstadt Vatican City
die Tschechoslowakei Czechoslovakia	Die Schweiz ist klein Switzerland is small.
die Türkei Turkey	Die Türkei ist groß. Turkey is large.

The names of most rivers in the German-speaking world are feminine *(die)*.

die Elbe the Elbe	die Havel the Havel
die Donau the Danube	die Weser the Weser
die Isar the Isar	

The following non-German rivers are also feminine *(die)*.

die Seine the Seine	die Wolga the Volga
die Themse the Thames	die Weichsel the Vistula

Most other rivers are masculine *(der)* in analogy with *der Fluß* ("river").

der Rhein	der Missouri
der Main	der Wisconsin
der Neckar	der Brahmaputra
der Mississippi	der Ganges

The days of the week, the months and the seasons of the year, as well as all words compounded with *der Tag* ("day") are masculine *(der)*.

der Mittwoch	Wednesday	der Herbst	autumn
der März	March	der Feiertag	holiday

Number (Plural)

The plural is formed in a number of ways. Nouns ending in *-e* usually add an *-n*.

die Tasche	die Taschen	pocket(s), bag(s), sack(s)
der Kunde	die Kunden	customer(s)
das Auge	die Augen	eye(s)

Many masculine *(der)* nouns add an *-e:*

der Tisch	die Tische	table(s)
der Tag	die Tage	day(s)
der Arm	die Arme	arm(s)

Most feminine *(die)* nouns add an *-en:*

die Tür	die Türen	door(s)
die Uhr	die Uhren	clock(s)
die Frau	die Frauen	woman (women)

A number of common nouns, both masculine *(der)* and feminine *(die)*, add an *-e* and an umlaut to the stem-vowel.

der Stuhl	die Stühle	chair(s)
der Zug	die Züge	train(s)
der Band	die Bände	volume(s) (of a book)
der Kopf	die Köpfe	head(s)
der Topf	die Töpfe	pot(s)
die Hand	die Hände	hand(s)
die Nacht	die Nächte	night(s)
die Wand	die Wände	wall(s)

Several masculine *(der)* and feminine *(die)* nouns form the plural by adding an umlaut to the stem-vowel.

der Mantel	die Mäntel	(over)coat(s)
der Garten	die Gärten	garden(s), yard(s)
der Vater	die Väter	father(s)
der Bruder	die Brüder	brother(s)
die Mutter	die Mütter	mother(s)
die Tochter	die Töchter	daughter(s)

Most masculine (*der*) and neuter (*das*) nouns ending in *-er* add nothing in the plural.

der Lehrer	die Lehrer	teacher(s)
der Arbeiter	die Arbeiter	worker(s)
das Fenster	die Fenster	window(s)
das Zimmer	die Zimmer	room(s)
das Laster	die Laster	moral vice(s)
der Lastwagen	die Lastwagen	truck(s)

Many common masculine (*der*) nouns referring to people add *-en*.*

der Mensch	die Menschen	human being(s)
der Pilot	die Piloten	pilot(s)
der Student	die Studenten	student(s)

*Note: With the exception of the dictionary (nominative) form, these nouns take an *-en* ending everywhere, even in the other cases of the singular. See discussion of Case to follow.

All feminine *(die)* nouns derived from the masculine counterpart and ending in *-in* add *-nen:*

die Lehrerin	die Lehrerinnen	teacher(s)
die Studentin	die Studentinnen	student(s), coed(s)
die Arbeiterin	die Arbeiterinnen	worker(s)

Several common masculine (*der*) and neuter (*das*) nouns add an *-er* and an umlaut to the stem-vowel in the plural.

der Mann	die Männer	man (men)
das Buch	die Bücher	book(s)
das Band	die Bänder	bands, ribbons
der Gott	die Götter	god(s)
das Dorf	die Dörfer	village(s)

Case

All German nouns and pronouns have markers that indicate case. There are four cases.

Nominative: the subject, used to identify objects, persons, places, etc. The nominative is the dictionary form of all nouns and pronouns.

| Das ist *der Zug/die Fahrkarte/das Gepäck.* | That is the train/the ticket/the luggage. |
| Das ist *ein Gepäckträger/eine Kellnerin/ein Kind.* | That is a porter/a waitress/a child. |

Accusative: the direct object of most transitive verbs; also follows the prepositions *bis* (until, up to), *durch* (through), *für* (for), *gegen* (against), *ohne* (without), and *um* (around). Note that accusative forms are exactly the same as nominative forms for feminine (*die*) and neuter (*das*) nouns and their equivalent pronouns.

Ich sehe *den Zug/die Fahrkarte/das Gepäck.*	I see the train/the ticket/the luggage.
Ich beobachte *einen Gepäckträger/ eine Kellnerin/ein Kind.*	I observe a porter/a waitress/a child.

In the plural, the accusative and nominative are also exactly the same.

Ich sehe die Züge/ die Gepäckträger/ die Kellnerinnen/ die Kinder.	I see the trains/ porters/ waitresses/ children.

Dative: the indirect object; also follows the prepositions *ab* (from this point on), *aus* (out of), *außer* (except), *bei* (at), *gegenüber* (opposite), *mit* (with), *nach* (after, towards), *seit* (since), *von* (of, from), and *zu* (to). Also, verbs such as *helfen* (to help), *schaden* (to injure), *zuhören* (to listen to), and a few others require dative objects.

Ich sage *dem Mann/der Frau/dem Kind* meine Meinung.	I tell the man/the woman/the child my opinion.
Ich gebe *einem Gepäckträger/einer Kellnerin ein Trinkgeld.*	I give a porter/a waitress a tip.
Ich helfe *dem Kind.*	I help the child.

Genitive: the possessive case; also follows the prepositions (*an*) *statt* (instead of), *trotz* (in spite of), *während* (during), *wegen* (because of), *innerhalb* (inside of), *außerhalb* (outside of), *oberhalb* (above), *unterhalb* (below).

Was ist der Preis *des (eines) Kugelschreibers/der (einer) Fahrkarte/des (eines) Buches?*	What is the price of the (of a) pen/of the (of a) ticket/of the (of a) book?

20. Prepositions

Like English, German has more than one hundred prepositions. In practice, however, only about two dozen are commonly used. German prepositions govern the accusative, dative, and genitive cases.

Accusative

The following prepositions always govern the accusative case:

bis until, up to
durch through
für for

gegen against
ohne without
um around (place); at (clock time)

Es ist schwer für dich. It is hard for you.
Er baut einen Zaun um den Garten. He is building a fence around the yard.

Note: *Bis* is rarely used in such a way as to reveal the accusative.

von Montag *bis* Mittwoch   from Monday to Wednesday
***bis* morgen**   until tomorrow
von zehn *bis* hundert   from ten to a hundred

Bis is frequently found linked with *zu* (plus dative), *auf* (plus accusative), *an* (plus accusative), or *nach* (plus dative).

bis zum nächsten Mal
bis auf mich
bis ans Ende der Welt
bis nach dem Spiel

until the next time
with the exception of me
to the end of the world
until after the game

Dative

The following prepositions always govern the dative case:

aus   out of
außer   except
bei   in the presence/home/business of
dank   thanks to
gegenüber   opposite, across from
mit   with
nach   to (with place names); after (in sequential order); according to
seit   since
von   of, from, by (passive agent)
zu   to

Von **wem hast du die Blumen?** Who did you get the flowers from?
Ich habe die Blumen *von* **dem Herrn Gerlach.** I got the flowers from Mr. Gerlach.

Genitive

The following prepositions usually govern the genitive:

(an)statt   instead of
trotz   in spite of
während   during
wegen   because of
bezüglich   with reference to
hinsichtlich   with regard to

angesichts   considering
außerhalb   outside (of)
innerhalb   inside (of)
oberhalb   above
unterhalb   beneath, below

(an)statt des Weines   instead of the wine
(an)statt meiner   instead of me
wegen des schlechten Wetters   because of the bad weather
wegen deiner   because of you

Formal written German requires the genitive with these prepositions. The informal spoken language, however, frequently uses them with the dative.

(an) statt mir   instead of me
wegen dir   because of you

Accusative/Dative

The following prepositions are frequently called *two-way prepositions* (in German: *Wechselpräpositionen*). They govern the dative when they indicate location in space or time. They govern the accusative when they indicate change of location. They usually govern the accusative when location or change of location is not literally implied by the verb.

Preposition	Dative	Accusative
an	at a vertical surface	towards a vertical surface
auf	on a horizontal surface	onto a horizontal surface
hinter	behind	going behind
in	in	into
neben	next to	moving next to
über	above	crossing over
unter	underneath	moving beneath; going under
vor	in front of, ago (with time)	crossing in front of
zwischen	in between	moving into the area between

Der Student kommt *in* das Zimmer. (accusative)	The student comes into the room.
Der Student sitzt zwei Stunden *im (in dem)* Zimmer. (dative)	The student sits for two hours in the room.
Der Student spricht *über das* Zimmer. (accusative)	The student is talking about the room.

Verbs of motion, such as *gehen, fahren, fallen, reisen,* and *kommen,* will often require one of these prepositions with the accusative.

Wir fahren *in* das Land der Belgier (nach Belgien). (accusative)	We are going to the land of the Belgians (to Belgium).
Wir besuchen Freunde *in* dem Land. (dative)	We are visiting friends in the land.
Er steigt *auf* den Berg. (accusative)	He is climbing (onto) the mountain.
Er steht *auf* dem Berg. (dative)	He is standing on the mountain.

Three pairs of verbs, *liegen/legen, sitzen/setzen,* and *stehen/stellen,* illustrate the difference between the dative and accusative use of these prepositions. The first verb in each pair indicates location, the second indicates change of location. *Liegen/legen* indicates location or horizontal movement, *sitzen/setzen* indicates sitting/setting, *stehen/stellen* indicates location or vertical movement.

Sie *legt* das Buch auf den Tisch.	She is putting the book on(to) the table.
Das Buch *liegt* auf dem Tisch.	The book is (lying) on the table.
Er *stellt* die Lampe in die Ecke.	He is putting (standing up) the lamp in(to) the corner.
Die Lampe *steht* in der Ecke.	The lamp is (standing) in the corner.

Note: *Liegen, sitzen,* and *stehen* are strong verbs. *Legen, setzen,* and *stellen* are weak verbs.

Contractions

A number of prepositions contract with the definite article that follows them.

an + dem	am	am Montag, am Fenster	on Monday, at the window
bei + dem	beim	beim Friseur	at the barber shop
in + dem	im	im Zimmer	in the room
in + das	ins	ins Zimmer	into the room
für + das	fürs	fürs Baby	for the baby
um + ums	ums	ums Herz	around the heart
von + dem	vom	vom Bahnhof	from the railroad station
zu + dem	zum	zum Beispiel	for example
zu + der	zur	zur Post	to the post office

These contractions are usually not separated except for emphasis.

am **Dienstag**	on Tuesday
an **dem Dienstag**	on that particular Tuesday
Du warst *beim* **Friseur.**	You were at the barber.
Du warst *bei dem* **Friseur!**	You were at that barber!

21. Adjectives and Adverbs

In German, adjectives and adverbs have many things in common. They have no characteristic form, unlike many English adverbs that have an "-ly" ending, as in "a quick bite" vs. "the dog runs quickly." They can, in most cases, be marked to indicate comparative or superlative degree. Compare English "more beautiful," "most beautiful" with "beautifully," "more beautifully," "most beautifully." They also modify other parts of speech. (Adjectives modify nouns; adverbs modify verbs, adjectives, and other adverbs.)

German adjectives, however, take endings that reflect gender, number, and case, like nouns. However, this happens only when they appear *before* the noun, not after it. Adjectives also have markers for comparative and superlative degree. German adverbs are marked only for comparative and superlative.

Adjectives

1. When an adjective follows a noun in a sentence, it has no special endings.

Das Buch ist blau.	The book is blue.
Der Bleistift ist gelb.	The pencil is yellow.
Die Tasche ist schwarz.	The bag is black.

When placed in front of the noun, however, adjectives take endings corresponding to gender, number, and case. The basic rule is: If there is no word like *der/die/das* or *ein/eine* present, the adjective(s) take(s) the ending regularly assigned to the *der/die/das* or *ein/eine* word:

blaues Buch	blue book
gelber Bleistift	yellow pencil
schwarze Tasche	black bag

2. The endings for the definite article, presented in Chapter 18, are the same as the endings on the adjectives.

	Singular			Plural
	Masculine	Feminine	Neuter	
Nominative	der	die	das	die
Accusative	den	die	das	die
Dative	dem	der	dem	den
Genitive	des	der	des	der

Separated out, the endings look like this:

	Masculine	Singular Feminine	Neuter	Plural
Nominative	-r	-e	-s	-e
Accusative	-n	-e	-s	-e
Dative	-m	-r	-m	-n
Genitive	-s(n*)	-r	-s(n*)	-r

*Note: Unpreceded adjectives in the genitive singular masculine and neuter have an *-n* instead of the *-s* that one would expect.
    Was ist der Preis des roten Weines? What is the price of the red wine?
    Was ist der Preis *roten* (not rotes) **Weines?** What is the price of red wine?

good wine	good milk	good bread	good friends
guter Wein	**gute Milch**	**gutes Brot**	**gute Freunde**
guten Wein	**gute Milch**	**gutes Brot**	**gute Freunde**
gutem Wein	**guter Milch**	**gutem Brot**	**guten Freunden**
guten Weines	**guter Milch**	**guten Brotes**	**guter Freunde**

3. When an adjective is preceded by an article or a word like an article (*der/die/das, ein/eine,* etc.), the adjectives take slightly different endings.

	Masculine	Singular Feminine	Neuter	Plural
Nominative	-e(r)	-e	-e(s)	-en
Accusative	-en	-e	-e(s)	-en
Dative	-en	-en	-en	-en
Genitive	-en	-en	-en	-en

the good wine	the good milk	the good bread	the good friends
der gute Wein	**die gute Milch**	**das gute Brot**	**die guten Freunde**
den guten Wein	**die gute Milch**	**das gute Brot**	**die guten Freunde**
dem guten Wein	**der guten Milch**	**dem guten Brot**	**den guten Freunden**
des guten Weines	**der guten Milch**	**des guten Brotes**	**der guten Freunde**
no good wine	no good milk	no good bread	no good friends
kein guter Wein	**keine gute Milch**	**kein gutes Brot**	**keine guten Freunde**
keinen guten Wein	**keine gute Milch**	**kein gutes Brot**	**keine guten Freunde**
keinem guten Wein	**keiner guten Milch**	**keinem guten Brot**	**keinen guten Freunden**
keines guten Weines	**keiner guten Milch**	**keinem guten Brot**	**keiner guten Freunde**

Comparison of Adjectives and Adverbs

1. All adjectives and adverbs have endings that indicate comparative ("more") and superlative ("most") degree.

    Comparative: **-er(-)**   Superlative: **-st(-)**

2. In the case of adjectives, the resulting forms are new adjectives that take the same endings as regular adjectives.

schön	beautiful	**schöner**	more beautiful	**schönst-**	most beautiful
klein	small	**kleiner**	smaller	**kleinst-**	smallest
dick	fat	**dicker**	fatter	**dickst-**	fattest

Multisyllabic adjectives form their comparative and superlative forms in the same way.

interessant	interesting	**interessanter**	more interesting	**interessantest**	most interesting
beliebt	beloved	**beliebter**	more beloved	**beliebtest**	most beloved
ausgezeichnet	excellent	**ausgezeichneter**	more excellent	**ausgezeichnetest**	most excellent

3. The *superlative* form as illustrated here cannot be used alone. It is possible to say:

Positive:
Dieses Buch ist klein.   This book is small.

Comparative:
Das Buch da ist kleiner.   That book is smaller.

But you must say:

Superlative:
Das ist das kleinste Buch.   That is the smallest book.

If, however, the superlative does not precede the noun, as in the last example above, either one of two ways of expressing the superlative adjective is possible. First of all, one can use the article plus the appropriate adjective *without* the noun. (English normally replaces the noun in question with the word "one(s).")

Das Buch ist das *kleinste* (Buch).   The book is the smallest (book) one.
Der Tisch ist der *teuerste* (Tisch).   The table is the most expensive (table) one.
Die Alpen sind die *schönsten* (Berge).   The Alps are the most beautiful (mountains) ones.

It is also possible to express the superlative by using *am ...-sten.*

Das Buch ist *am* klein*sten*.   The book is the smallest.
Der Tisch ist *am* teuer*sten*.   The table is the most expensive.
Die Bluse ist *am* neue*sten*.   The blouse is the newest.
Die Alpen sind *am* schön*sten*.   The Alps are the most beautiful.

Adverbs

Adverbs like *hier* ("here"), *dort* ("there"), *jetzt* ("now"), *nie* ("never"), *sehr* ("very"), *ziemlich* ("quite," "rather"), etc., are like their English counterparts. Adjectives that function like adverbs, such as *schön* ("beautifully"), *schnell* ("quickly"), *ruhig* ("peacefully"), *gut* ("well"), and *schlecht* ("poorly," "badly") can be marked for comparative and superlative just like adjectives. However, only the form marked *am...-sten* can be used for adverbs in the superlative.

schnell, schneller, am schnellsten	fast, faster, fastest
schlecht, schlechter, am schlechtesten	bad, worse, worst
freundlich, freundlicher, am freundlichsten	friendly, friendlier, friendliest

Irregular Adjectives and Adverbs

alt, älter, ältest-/am ältesten	old, older, oldest
arm, ärmer, ärmest-/am ärmsten	poor, poorer, poorest
bald, eher, am ehesten (adverb only)	soon, sooner, soonest
dumm, dümmer, dümmst-/am dümmsten	dumb, dumber, dumbest
gut, besser, best-/am besten	good (well), better, best
hart, härter, härtest	hard, harder, hardest
jung, jünger, jüngst-/am jüngsten	young, younger, youngest
rot, röter, rötest-/am rötesten	red, redder, reddest
schwach, schwächer, schwächst-/am schwächsten	weak, weaker, weakest
schwarz, schwärzer, schwärzest-/am schwärzesten	black, blacker, blackest
klug, klüger, klügst-/am klügsten	smart, smarter, smartest
lang, länger, längst-/am längsten	long, longer, longest
kurz, kürzer, kürzest-/am kürzesten	short, shorter, shortest
stark, stärker, stärkst-/am stärksten	strong, stronger, strongest
gesund, gesünder, gesündest-/am gesündesten	healthy, healthier, healthiest
groß, größer, größt-/am größten	big/great, bigger/greater, biggest/greatest
hoch, höher, höchst-/am höchsten	high/tall, higher/taller, highest/tallest
nah, näher, nächst-/am nächsten	near, nearer, nearest
kalt, kälter, kältest-/am kältesten	cold, colder, coldest
warm, wärmer, wärmst-/am wärmsten	warm, warmer, warmest

Gern

The irregular adverb *gern* is used to indicate a liking or preference for a particular activity.

gern, lieber, am liebsten*

Gern makes a verb into the equivalent of "like to."

Ich schreibe Briefe.	I write letters.
Ich schreibe gern Briefe.	I like to write letters.
Er arbeitete dort.	He worked there.
Er arbeitete gern dort.	He liked to work there.
Wir wären gekommen.	We would have come.
Wir wären gern gekommen.	We would have gladly come.

Lieber indicates the equivalent of "prefer to."

Er schreibt gern, aber er liest lieber.	He likes to write but he prefers to read.
Wir wären gern gekommen, aber wir hätten euch lieber zu uns eingeladen.	We would have liked to come, but we would have preferred to invite you over to our place.

Am liebsten means "most of all."

Ich trinke Cola gern, Bier lieber, aber Wein am liebsten.	I like to drink Coke, prefer beer, but like wine most of all.
W.C. Fields wäre am liebsten in Philadelphia gewesen.	W.C. Fields would have liked being in Philadelphia most of all.

*Note: *Gern* should not be confused with *lieb*, meaning "dear," "kind," "nice," which has the same comparative and superlative forms, *lieber, liebst-/am liebsten*, but which is an adjective, not an adverb.

22. Numbers

Numbers are adjectives that normally do not take any endings. The notable exception is *ein*, which means "one" or "a/an." It takes the same endings as *kein/keine*, which was illustrated in the previous chapter.

	Masculine	Feminine	Neuter
Nominative	ein	eine	ein
Accusative	einen	eine	ein
Dative	einem	einer	einem
Genitive	eines	einer	eines

Cardinal Numbers

1. The cardinal numbers in German are as follows.

0	null	zero	31	einunddreißig	thirty-one
1	eins	one	40	vierzig	forty
2	zwei	two	42	zweiundvierzig	forty-two
3	drei	three	50	fünfzig	fifty
4	vier	four	53	dreiundfünfzig	fifty-three
5	fünf	five	60	sechzig	sixty
6	sechs	six	64	vierundsechzig	sixty-four
7	sieben	seven	70	siebzig	seventy
8	acht	eight	75	fünfundsiebzig	seventy-five
9	neun	nine	80	achtzig	eighty
10	zehn	ten	86	sechsundachtzig	eighty-six
11	elf	eleven	90	neunzig	ninety
12	zwölf	twelve	97	siebenundneunzig	ninety-seven
13	dreizehn	thirteen	100	(ein)hundert	one hundred
14	vierzehn	fourteen	108	(ein)hundertacht	one hundred and eight
15	fünfzehn	fifteen	200	zweihundert	two hundred
16	sechszehn	sixteen	209	zweihundertneun	two hundred and nine
17	siebzehn	seventeen	900	neunhundert	nine hundred
18	achtzehn	eighteen	1.000	tausend	one thousand
19	neunzehn	nineteen	3.000	dreitausend	three thousand
20	zwanzig	twenty	1.000.000	eine Million	one million
21	einundzwanzig	twenty-one	8.000.000	acht Millionen	eight million
22	zweiundzwanzig	twenty-two	1.000.000.000	eine Milliarde	one billion
23	dreiundzwanzig	twenty-three	4.000.000.000	vier Milliarden	four billion
24	vierundzwanzig	twenty-four	1.000.000.000.000	eine Billion	one trillion
25	fünfundzwanzig	twenty-five			
26	sechsundzwanzig	twenty-six			
27	siebenundzwanzig	twenty-seven			
28	achtundzwanzig	twenty-eight			
29	neunundzwanzig	twenty-nine			
30	dreißig	thirty			

The numbers not listed follow the pattern set up for the numbers between *zwanzig* and *dreißig*.

2. Large numbers are usually written with a space or a period (.) where English uses a comma (,), and with a comma where English uses a period. Thus, 158,497.62 is written in German as either 158 497,62 or 158.497,62. It is read in German *hundertachtundfünfzigtausend vierhundertsiebenundneunzig Komma zweiundsechzig*.

3. The names of cardinal numbers can be used as nouns. They are feminine (*die*) when so used:

die Eins the (number) one   **die Zehn** the (number) ten
die Sechs the (number) six   **die Hundert** the (number) hundred

Ordinal Numbers

1. The ordinal numbers in German are as follows.

erst-	first	einundzwanzigst-	twenty-first
zweit-	second	zweiundzwanzigst-	twenty-second
dritt-	third	dreiundzwanzigst-	twenty-third
viert-	fourth	vierundzwanzigst-	twenty-fourth
fünft-	fifth	fünfundzwanzigst-	twenty-fifth
sechst-	sixth	sechsundzwanzigst-	twenty-sixth
siebt-	seventh	siebenundzwanzigst-	twenty-seventh
acht-	eighth	achtundzwanzigst-	twenty-eighth
neunt-	ninth	neunundzwanzigst-	twenty-ninth
zehnt-	tenth	dreißigst-	thirtieth
elft-	eleventh	einunddreißigst-	thirty-first
zwölft-	twelfth	vierzigst-	fortieth
dreizehnt-	thirteenth	fünfzigst-	fiftieth
vierzehnt-	fourteenth	sechzigst-	sixtieth
fünfzehnt-	fifteenth	siebzigst-	seventieth
sechzehnt-	sixteenth	achtzigst-	eightieth
siebzehnt-	seventeenth	neunzigst-	ninetieth
achtzehnt-	eighteenth	hundertest-	hundredth
neunzehnt-	nineteenth	tausendst-	thousandth
zwanzigst-	twentieth	letzt-	last

2. Like other adjectives, ordinal numbers take endings that indicate gender, number, and case.

der erste Mensch the first human being
mein drittes Wörterbuch my third dictionary
zum fünfzehnten Mal for the fifteenth time

3. When ordinals are written as numerals, they are always followed by a period (.).

    Heute ist der 18. Juli.   Today is the 18th of July.
    In diesem Jahr feiern wir den 208.   This year we are celebrating the 208th
    Geburtstag der USA.   birthday of the USA.

4. When indicating the order of accession to a royal throne or nobility of birth, German uses the given name followed by the ordinal number with appropriate endings for gender and case:

    Wilhelm II. = Wilhelm der Zweite   William II/William the Second
    Ich kenne Wilhelm den Zweiten.   I know William the Second.
    Er war ein Freund von Wilhelm dem Zweiten.   He was a friend of William the Second.
    Das ist das Schloß Wilhelms des Zweiten.   That is William the Second's castle.

Fractions

In reading fractions, the numerator is a cardinal number ("one," *ein*). The denominator is an ordinal number with the ending *-el*. The result is a phrase with a number and a noun that does *not* change form when it becomes plural.

    ein Drittel   1/3
    zwei Drittel   2/3
    ein Viertel   1/4
    zwei Fünftel   2/5
    sechs Zwanzigstel   6/20
    dreizehn Neununddreißigstel   13/39
    siebenundfünfzig Einhundertneunundneunzigstel   57/199

"One half" is *eine Hälfte* (plural, *Hälften*). "Half of" is *die Hälfte von* or *die Hälfte* followed by the genitive. "A half (of) a(n)" is *ein(e) halbe(r)(s)*.

    eine Hälfte der Gruppe   one half of the group
    beide Hälften der Kugel   both halves of the ball (sphere)
    die Hälfte der Studenten   half of the students
    die Hälfte vom (von dem) Kuchen   half of the cake
    ein halbes Hähnchen   a half a chicken
    eine halbe Zwiebel   a half an onion

With other numbers, "and a half" is *einhalb*.

    zweieinhalb   2 1/2
    fünfeinhalb   5 1/2

"One and a half" (1 1/2) is *anderthalb* or *eineinhalb*.

Arithmetic

\+ (das Pluszeichen) *plus* (the plus sign) **plus**

2 + 3 = 5 zwei *plus* drei gleicht (ist, macht) fünf
9 + 6 = 15 neun *plus* sechs gleicht (ist, macht) fünfzehn

− (das Minuszeichen) *minus, weniger* (the minus sign) **minus, less**

16 − 9 = 7 sechszehn *minus* neun ist (gleicht, macht) sieben
8 − 8 = 0 acht *minus* acht ist (gleicht, macht) null

× (das Multiplikationszeichen) *mal* (the multiplication sign) **times**

5 × 3 = 15 fünf *mal* drei macht (gleicht, ist) fünfzehn
6 × 4 = 24 sechs *mal* vier macht (gleicht, ist) vierundzwanzig

÷ (das Divisionszeichen) *geteilt durch* (the division sign) **divided by**

9 ÷ 3 = 3 neun *geteilt* durch drei ist drei
30 ÷ 6 = 5 dreißig *geteilt* durch sechs ist fünf

= (das Gleichzeichen) *gleicht (ist, macht)* (the equal sign) **equals**

23. Demonstrative Adjectives

Demonstrative adjectives indicate information such as location, number, and quality. They correspond to the English "this," "that," "those," "each," "all," "which," "such a(n)," etc. Most German demonstrative adjectives are inflected for gender, number, and case. They can be used either alone or in front of the noun in question. In the lists that follow, singular forms are separated from plural forms by a double slash (//).

der, die, das//die	the; that//those*
dieser, diese, dieses//diese	this//these
welcher, welche, welches//welche	which (one//ones)?
mancher, manche, manches//manche	many a(n)//many
jeder, jede, jedes	each, every (no plural)
alles//alle	everything, all//all, all of
so ein, so eine, so ein//solche**	such a(n)//such...like that//those
viel***	much of something, a lot of something
vieles	much, a lot (pronoun)
viele	many, a lot of things, people, ideas, etc.
einige	a few, some
wenig***	little, not much
wenige	few, not many
mehrere	several
mehr***	more (of an object or objects)
weniger	less
etwas***	something, some
jemand	someone, somebody
irgendein, irgendeine//irgenwelche	any (at all)
der meiste, die meiste, das meiste//die meisten	most (of the)

*Note: Although the older word *jener, jene, jenes//jene* is still found in written German, it is rarely used in modern spoken German. To distinguish between "this" and "that" in German use *dieser, diese, dieses//diese* for "this/these" and *der, die, das//die* (intensified by a word such as *da* or *dort* ("there")) for "that//those." **Meinst du dieses Buch (hier) oder das Buch (dort drüben)?** Do you mean this book (here) or that book (over there)?

***Solcher, solche, solches//solche* is also possible.

***Mehr and *etwas* are not inflected. *Viel* and *wenig* are inflected only when they are used in an adjective phrase.

Viel Wein kostet viel Geld.	A lot of wine costs a lot of money.
Mit dem vielen Wein kann man sich gut betrinken	With that much wine you can get very drunk.

Das

The pronoun *das* is a universal demonstrative. It is often used without reference to gender or number. It can be translated as "that//those" or "this//these."

Was ist das?	What is that (this)?
Das ist ein Tisch.	That is a table
Das ist eine Tasche.	That is a bag.
Das ist ein Fenster.	That is a window.
Was sind das?	What are those (these) things?
Das sind Tische.	Those (These) are tables.
Wer ist das?	Who is that?
Das ist mein Onkel.	That is my uncle.

24. Possessive Adjectives and Pronouns

Possessive adjectives operate much like demonstrative adjectives, in that they can 1) stand alone (like pronouns) or 2) be placed in front of their respective noun. As a result, there are really two sets of related forms, one for use in front of the noun and one for use alone. In the lists below, the singular and plural forms are separated by a double slash (//). Possessive adjectives and pronouns are inflected for gender, number, and case. (See *kein*, p. 74, and *ein*, p. 78.)

The following forms are used before adjectives and nouns.

mein, meine, mein//meine	my____
dein, deine, dein//deine	your____
sein, seine, sein//seine	his____, its____
ihr (Ihr), ihr (Ihre), ihr (Ihr)//ihre (Ihre)	her____, their____, (your____)
unser, unsere, unser//unsere	our____
euer, eu(e)re, euer//eu(e)re	your____

The following forms are used alone as pronouns.

meiner, meine, meines//meine	mine
deiner, deine, deines//deine	yours
seiner, seine//seines//seine	his
ihrer (Ihrer), ihre (Ihre), ihres (Ihres)//ihre (Ihre)	hers, theirs, (yours)
unserer, unsere, unseres//unsere	ours
eu(e)rer, eu(e)re, eu(e)res//eu(e)re	yours

25. Object Pronouns

1. Subject pronouns were introduced in Chapter 2. All personal pronouns have forms that indicate the accusative, dative, and genitive. The object pronouns are

	Singular		Plural	
Nominative:	ich	I	wir	we
Accusative:	mich	me	uns	us
Dative:	mir	to me	uns	to us
Genitive:	meiner*	of me	unser*	of us
Nominative:	du	you	ihr	you
Accusative:	dich	you	euch	you
Dative:	dir	to you	euch	to you
Genitive:	deiner*	of you	euer*	of you
Nominative:	er	he	sie	they
	sie	she	es	it
Accusative:	ihn	him	sie	them
	sie	her	es	it
Dative:	ihm	to him	ihnen	to them
	ihr	to her	ihm	to it
Genitive:	seiner*		ihrer*	
	ihrer*		seiner*	

*Note: The genitive pronouns are rarely used in modern German.

2. The object pronouns are used in exactly the same way as corresponding nouns, with one qualification. After a preposition, a pronoun is normally used only if it refers to a person.

für mich	for me
mit dir	with you
außer ihm	except for him
bei ihr	at her place
ohne sie	without her/them
von uns	from/of us

3. When the pronoun idea involved refers to an inanimate object, a compound involving the word *da-* (*dar-* preceding a vowel) is used.

auf dem Tisch   on the table
darauf   on it

in der Tasche   in the pocket
darin   in it

vor der Schule in front of the school
davor in front (of it)

hinter den Häusern behind the houses
dahinter behind them

zwischen dem Haus und der Schule between the house and the school
dazwischen between (them)

4. Each *da-/dar-*word has a corresponding question form with *wo-? (wor-?* before a vowel).

Worüber sprechen Sie heute?	What are you speaking about today?
Ich sprechen über die Inflation in Argentinien.	I am speaking about inflation in Argentina.
Ich spreche *darüber*.	I am speaking about it.
Woran denkst du?	What are you thinking about?
Ich denke an einen Tag in Mai.	I am thinking about a day in May.
Ich denke *daran*.	I am thinking about it.

5. Note that not every preposition plus pronoun can be replaced by a *da-/dar-*compound. The prepositions below are replaced by the following compounds listed in boldface.

ohne	**ohne, ohnedies**	("without it")
bis	**bis dahin**	("until then")
außer	**außerdem**	("besides" "in addition")
seit	**seitdem**	("since" as an adverb)
statt	**stattdessen**	("instead")
trotz	**trotzdem**	("nevertheless")
während	**währenddessen**	("in the meanwhile")
wegen	**deswegen**	("for that reason")

6. In addition to the pronouns above, the articles *der/die/das* are frequently used as pronouns, as substitutes for *er/sie/es*. This renders the pronoun idea emphatic.

Der kann gut reden!	*He* should talk!
Was gibst du mir für *die*?	What will you give me for *them*?
Die sieht aber gut aus!	Does *she* ever look good!

7. Note that the pronouns always take the case appropriate to the sentence, even if the sentence is incomplete.

Wer ist da?	Who is there?
Ich (bin es)!	Me (lit.: I am it)!
Wen meinst du?	Who(m) do you mean?
Dich (meine ich)!	You (I mean)!
Wer soll gehen?	Who is supposed to go?
Du (sollst gehen)!	You (are supposed to go)!
Wem gibst du das Geld?	To whom are you giving the money?
Mir!	(To) Me!
Wer ist gekommen?	Who came?
Er!	He did!

26. Reflexive Pronouns

1. The term *reflexive* refers to a situation in which the subject and one of the objects in a sentence are the same. English has reflexives:

> I saw *myself* in the mirror.
> She talks to *herself* all the time.
> He buys *himself* only the best clothes.
> We cannot imagine *ourselves* living anywhere else.

2. The object pronouns discussed in the previous chapter also serve as reflexive pronouns.

Nominative:	**ich**	I	**wir**	we
Accusative:	**mich**	myself	**uns**	ourselves
Dative:	**mir**	to myself	**uns**	to ourselves
Genitive:	**meiner**	of myself	**unser**	of ourselves*
Nominative:	**du**	you	**ihr**	you
Accusative:	**dich**	yourself	**euch**	yourselves
Dative:	**dir**	to yourself	**euch**	to yourselves
Genitive:	**deiner**	of yourself	**euer**	of yourselves*

Ich sehe *mich* im Spiegel.   I see myself in the mirror.
Wir sehen *uns* jeden Tag.   We see each other every day.

*Note: See note in Chapter 25 about the use of the genitive.

In the third person, singular and plural, as well as for *Sie,* a single pronoun is used for reflexive constructions, namely *sich.*

Er fragt *sich* das oft.   He often asks himself that.
Sie kaufen *sich* Wein.   They/You buy themselves/yourself (yourselves) wine.

3. If a verb can take an object, it usually *must* take one, even if the object must be reflexive. As a result, there are many reflexive verbs in German whose counterparts in English are not reflexive.

erinnern (an + accusative)   to remind (of)
sich erinnern (an + accusative)   to remember

interessiern (für + accusative)   to interest (in)
sich interessieren (für + accusative)   to be interested (in)

einigen	to unite two opinions
sich einigen (über + accusative)	to agree (about)
finden	to find
sich befinden	to be located
fühlen	to feel (touch) something
sich fühlen	to feel a certain emotion or sensation
fragen	to ask
sich fragen	to wonder (to ask oneself)
lieben	to love
sich verlieben (in + accusative)	to fall in love (with)
wundern	to amaze
sich wundern	to be amazed

27. Relative Pronouns

1. The relative pronouns in English are "that," "who," "whom," "whose," and "which."

> Who was that man (*whom*) I saw you with last night?
> These are the times *that* try men's souls.
> Have you seen the new film (*that is*) playing in town?

2. German has a complete set of relative pronouns, with forms for gender, number, and case. The relative pronouns are basically the definite article *der/die/das* with some minor modifications in the genitive and dative cases.

	Masculine	Singular Feminine	Neuter	Plural
Nominative:	**der**	**die**	**das**	**die**
Accusative:	**den**	**die**	**das**	**die**
Dative:	**dem**	**der**	**dem**	**denen**
Genitive:	**dessen**	**deren**	**dessen**	**deren**

3. In selecting the appropriate relative pronoun, the gender and number are determined by the gender and number of the antecedent (the word referred back to in the first sentence). The case is determined by the case of the word in the second sentence.

Das Buch ist schwarz.	The book is black.
Das Buch liegt auf dem Tisch.	The book is lying on the table.
Das Buch, *das* **auf dem Tisch liegt, ist schwarz.**	The book that is (lying) on the table is black.
Der Stuhl steht am Fenster.	The chair is in front of the window.
Ich sehe den Stuhl.	I see the table.
Der Stuhl, *den* **ich sehe, steht am Fenster.**	The chair that I see is in front of the window.
Die Tasche kostet zu viel.	The purse costs too much.
Ich gebe Ihnen zwei Mark für die Tasche.	I'll give you two Marks for the purse.
Die Tasche, *für die* **ich Ihnen zwei Mark gebe, kostet zuviel.**	The purse that I'll give you two Marks for, costs too much.
Der Student heißt Markus.	The student is named Markus.
Seine Noten sind gut.	His grades are good.
Der Student, *dessen* **Noten gut sind, heißt Markus.**	The student whose grades are good is named Markus.

Note: *Dessen/deren* are usually translated as "whose."

Die Bücher, *deren* Umschläge aus Leder sind, sind sehr alt.	The books *whose* covers are (made) of leather are very old.
Der Mann, *dessen* Auto kaputt ist, weint.	The man *whose* car is wrecked is crying.

4. The verb after a relative pronoun goes at the end of its clause, and the relative pronoun is placed at the front of the clause. If the relative pronoun is part of a prepositional phrase, the preposition stays in front of its pronoun. In such cases, the relative pronoun *must* be used. It cannot be left out, as is often the case in English.

Wer war die Frau, mit der ich dich gestern abend gesehen habe?	Who was that woman (whom) I saw you with last night?
Wie heißt der Roman, den du mir empfohlen hast?	What is the name of that novel (that) you told me to read?
Das ist ein Film, den du sehen sollst.	That is a film (that) you ought to see.
Hier ist das Zimmer, das Sie am Telefon reserviert haben.	Here is the room (that) you reserved over the phone.

28. Negatives

Nicht

1. The most common negative in German is *nicht* ("not"). It is placed *after* a verb, but normally *before* other parts of speech.

Meine Uhr geht *nicht*.	My watch does not work.
Es ist *nicht* meine Uhr.	It is not my watch.
Meine Uhr ist *nicht* alt.	My watch is not old.
Deine Uhr funktioniert *nicht* besonders gut.	Your watch does not function especially well.

2. The placement of *nicht* is otherwise determined by the emphasis the speaker or writer wishes to give an utterance.

Er ist heute abend *nicht* zu Hause.	He is not home this evening.
Wir waren vorigen Sommer *nicht* in Chicago.	We were not in Chicago last summer.

It is also possible for *nicht* to be the last element in a simple sentence. Normally *nicht* will follow an expression of time but precede an expression of place.

Die Studenten studieren heutzutage *nicht*.	(The) students do not study nowadays.
Die Studenten studieren *nicht* in der Universität.	(The) students do not study in the university.

3. *Nicht* is found at the beginning of a sentence only if it modifies a (pro)noun or adjective or adverb already there. It cannot stand alone at the beginning of a sentence.

Nicht ich, sondern wir, gehen.	Not I, but we, are going.
Nicht rot, sondern schwarz, war das Telefon.	Not red, but black, was the telephone.

Kein/keine

Most nouns are negated by means of the demonstrative adjective *kein/keine*, which is inflected exactly like *mein/meine, dein/deine, sein/seine,* and *ihr/ihre (Ihr/Ihre)*.

	Singular			Plural
	Masculine	Feminine	Neuter	
Nominative:	kein	keine	kein	keine
Accusative:	keinen	keine	kein	keine
Dative:	keinem	keiner	keinem	keinen
Genitive:	keines	keiner	keines	keiner

Kein/keine corresponds to English "not a(n), not any, no..."

Nein, ich haben *keinen* (Bleistift). No, I do not (have a pencil).
Es gibt *keine* Wolken am Himmel. There are no clouds in the sky.
Das sind *keine* Wolken, das ist Nebel. Those are not clouds, that is fog.

Other Negatives

In addition to *nicht* and *kein/keine* there are a number of pronouns and adverbs that carry a negative meaning:

nichts nothing
niemand nobody, no one
nirgends nowhere
nirgendwohin (to) nowhere
nie never

Ich gehe *nie* ins Kino. I never go to the movies.
***Niemand* will das Geschirr abwaschen.** Nobody wants to wash the dishes.
Man kann *nichts* dafür. You can't do anything about it.

Sondern

The conjuction *sondern* is used to neutralize a negative statement. It corresponds to the English "but" used in the sense of "but on the other hand" or "but rather."

Das ist kein Telefonbuch, *sondern* ein Katalog. That is not a telephone book, but a catalogue.
Ich faulenze nicht, *sondern* ich arbeite langsam! I'm not goofing off, but working slowly!
Du bist nicht nur faul, *sondern* auch frech! You are not only lazy, but impudent as well!

29. Interrogatives and Exclamations

1. The most common interrogatives in German are:

Welcher?/Welche?/Welches?	Which?	**Wieso?**	How come? Why?
Wer?	Who?	**Warum?**	Why?
Wen?	Whom? (accusative)	**Wann?**	When?
Wem?	(to) Whom? (dative)	**Wo?**	Where?
Wessen?	Whose? (genitive; rarely used)	**Woher?**	Where (do you come/are you coming) from?
Was?	What?	**Wohin?**	Where (are you going) to?
Wie?	How?		

Was gibt es zum Essen? — What are we having to eat?
Wohin willst du morgen? — Where do you want to go tomorrow?
Wieso willst du nichts essen? — How come you don't want to eat anything?
Woher kommt das Fleisch? — Where does this meat come from?

Note: Only *welcher* and *wer* are inflected for case. For the inflection of *welcher*, see *kein/keine* on page 92.

2. German has a number of "flavor" words that cannot always be translated readily into English.

doch! — yes, of course (used to counteract a negative statement)
Er ist gestern nicht nach Hause gekommen. — He did not come home yesterday.
***Doch!* Er ist *doch* nach Hause gekommen.** — Yes, he did (too)! He *did* come home.

ja! — really (used for emphasis)
Es ist *ja* kalt! — It really is cold!

aber! — (is it) ever (used for emphasis)
Mensch, ist es aber kalt! — Man, is it ever cold!

denn! — (well) then (used to indicate impatience)
Wie heißt du *denn*? — What, then, is your name?
Was ist *denn* das? — What on earth is that?

gerade — right now (conveys immediacy)
Was machen Sie *gerade*? — What are you doing right now?

nur, bloß — only, just
Das Buch kostet *nur (bloß)* fünf Dollar! — The book costs only (just) five dollars!
Denken Sie nur, es kostet *bloß (nur)* fünf Dollar! — Just think, it costs only (just) five dollars!

30. Practical Sentence Rules

Sentence Types

There are three basic kinds of sentences in German, all described in terms of the position of the inflected verb. There are two "main sentence" or "main clause" types (*Hauptsatz/Hauptsätze*) and one "subordinate sentence" or "subordinate clause" type *(Nebensatz/Nebensätze).*

Main Sentences/Clauses

1. The *Hauptsätze* include the statement *(Aussagesatz)*, the question *(Fragesatz)*, and the imperative *(Befehl)* sentence. In a statement, the subject usually comes first. The conjugated verb is, however, *always* the second element in the sentence.

Ich *komme* nach Hause.	I am coming home.
Der Student *schreibt* einen Aufsatz.	The student is writing a composition.
Mathias und Anna *haben* vorige Woche geheiratet.	Matthew and Ann got married last week.
Wir *möchten* jetzt gehen.	We would like to go now.

2. Often in German some element other than the subject is placed first in the sentence. The conjugated verb is *still* the second element.

So etwas *habe* ich oft gesagt.	I have often said things like that.
Meiner Großmutter *schreibt* unser Vater jetzt einen Brief.	Our father is writing my grandmother a letter right now.
Wenn ich eine Million Dollar hätte, *würde* ich mir ein großes Haus bauen lassen.	If I had a million dollars, I would have a big house built.

3. In a question, the conjugated verb is placed *first* in the sentence if the question is a "yes/no" *(ja/nein)* question. If it is not a "yes/no" question, the verb is placed directly after the question word (*Was? Wer? Wen? Wem? Wo? Wann? Warum?* etc.).

Willst du mit uns gehen?	Do you want to go with us?
Hat er dich gesehen?	Did he see you?
Sehen wir uns nächste Woche?	Will we see each other next week?
Was *machst* du gerade?	What are you doing right now?
Wann *kommt* er nach Hause?	When is he coming home?
Warum *müssen* wir diese Prüfung machen?	Why do we have to do this exam?

4. In commands, the imperative form of the verb comes first.

Kommen Sie sofort!
Macht eure Hausaufgaben!
Sag das bitte nicht!

Come immediately!
Do your homework!
Please don't say that!

Subordinate Sentences/Clauses

Nebensätze include all clauses that begin with a so-called *subordinating conjunction*. Subordinating conjunctions include 1) all relative pronouns, 2) all question-words used in an indirect statement ("He didn't tell us, *when* he was coming."), and 3) the following words:

daß	that	**da**	since, because
wenn	if, whenever	**seit (dem)**	since
weil	because	**nachdem**	after
als ob	as if	**während**	while
obwohl	although	**auch wenn**	even if
als	when (single event in the past)		

Ich weiß nicht, *wann* er zu uns kommen *wird*.
Er hat uns gestern geschrieben, *daß* er erst übermorgen abreisen *kann*.
Er ist der Onkel, *den* du vorigen Sommer in Chicago kennengelernt *hast*.

I don't know, when he will come over (to our house).
He wrote us yesterday, that he cannot leave until the day after tomorrow.
He is the uncle (whom) you met last summer in Chicago.

Second Position, Last Position

The conjugated verb is always second in a statement or a question beginning with a question-word. It is first in "yes/no" questions. It is last in subordinate clauses. If the verb has a *complement,* such as a separable prefix or an infinitive, that element comes *last* in the given clause, except where the conjugated verb would come last.

Wir *fangen* pünktlich um neun Uhr *an*.
Er hat soeben gesagt, daß wir pünktlich um neun Uhr *anfangen*.
Ich *möchte* gerne eine Tasse Kaffee mit Milch *bestellen*.
Ich wiederhole, daß ich gerne eine Tasse Kaffee mit Milch *bestellen möchte!*
Die Schüler *haben* ihre Hausaufgaben sehr schön *gemacht*.
Der Lehrer war immer sehr froh, wenn die Schüler ihre Hausaufgaben sehr schön *gemacht haben*.

We begin promptly at nine o'clock.
He just said, that we begin promptly at nine o'clock.
I would like to order a cup of coffee with milk.
I repeat, that I would like to order a cup of coffee with milk!
The pupils (students) did their homework very nicely.
The teacher was always very happy, when (ever) the pupils did their homework very nicely.

Time, Manner, Place

1. Expressions of time come before expressions of place. This is the exact opposite of what happens in English.

>Ich komme um fünf Uhr nach Hause. I'm coming home at five o'clock.
>Wir haben uns vorige Woche in Boston We met in Boston last week.
>kennengelernt.

2. If expressions of time, manner, and place were to be found in the same sentence, the line up would be time, manner, place.

>Wir fahren sonntags gern auf das Land. We enjoy driving to the country on Sundays.

31. Suffixes

A number of suffixes carry special meanings. The most common are:

-t/-en   found on all past participles

-er   -er (a male who performs some action)
der Arbeiter   worker

-in   -er, -ess (a female who peforms some action)
die Arbeiterin   worker

-ung   -ing (an abstraction of an action)
die Übung   exercising, exercise
die Täuschung   illusion
die Befreiung   liberation, freeing

-heit/-keit   -hood, -ty
die Schönheit   beauty
die Einheit   unit, unity
die Feuchtigkeit   humidity
die Mannigfaltigkeit   variety

-(")e   -ness (the quality of something)
die Güte   goodness, quality
das Richtige   that which is correct, right
die Treue   faithfulness

-ieren   a verb suffix of French origin found in many foreign verbs
studieren   study
diskutieren   discuss
konsultieren   consult
regulieren   regulate

-schaft   -ship
die Freundschaft   friendship

-bar   -ble
eßbar   edible
machbar   feasible
furchtbar   terrible
annehmbar   acceptable
ausdehnbar   expandable

-tum   -dom
der Reichtum   wealth
das Irrtum   error

-los   -less ("without")
kinderlos   childless
furchtlos   fearless
machtlos   powerless
glaslos   without glass
arbeitslos   without work, unemployed

-ig   -y
ruhig   quiet, quietly

-isch   -y
typisch   typical

-ei   -y
die Partei   (political) party

-ie   -y
die Harmonie   harmony

-erei   -ry
die Bäckerei   bakery
die Molkerei   dairy
die Gießerei   foundry

The suffix *-erei* is frequently attached to the stem of a verb to make fun of the activity in question.

die Lauferei   (useless) running around
die Fragerei   asking (foolish) questions
die Fliegerei   flying around (all the time!)

32. Time

Times of the Day

der Tag, -e day, days
täglich daily
Tages- daily (*used in compound words, such as* **Tageszeitung**, *"daily newspaper."*)
der Vormittag morning, forenoon
der Nachmittag afternoon

der Mittag noontime (*not necessarily 12:00 p.m.*)
die Nacht, Nächte night, nights
die Mitternacht midnight
der Abend, -e evening, evenings

Days of the Week

die Woche, -n week, weeks
wöchentlich weekly
Wochen- weekly (*used in compound words, such as* **Wochenzeitschrift**, *"weekly magazine."*)
der Montag Monday
der Dienstag Tuesday
der Mittwoch Wednesday
der Donnerstag Thursday
der Freitag Friday
der Samstag Saturday
(der Sonnabend) (*Alternate term for "Saturday" in the North and East of Germany*)
der Sonntag Sunday

am (an dem) Freitag on Friday
am Dienstag on Tuesday
am Mittwoch on Wednesday
jeden Sonntag every Sunday
jeden Donnerstag every Thursday
jeden Samstag every Saturday
nächsten Sonntag next Sunday
letzten Donnerstag last Thursday
vorigen Samstag last (*the previous*) Saturday
montags Mondays, every Monday
mittwochs Wednesdays, every Wednesday
freitags Fridays, every Friday

Months

der Monat, -e month, months
monatlich monthly
Monats- monthly (*used in compound words, such as* **Monatskarte**, *"monthly ticket."*)
der Januar January
(der Jänner) (*Alternate term for "January" in Austria*)
der Februar February
(der Feber) (*Alternate term for "February" in Austria*)

der März March
der April April
der Mai May
der Juni June
der Juli July
der August August
der September September
der Oktober October
der November November
der Dezember December

Seasons

im (in dem) Mai   in May
im Oktober   in October
jeden Februar   every February
jeden März   every March
nächsten April   next April
die Jahreszeit, -en   season, seasons
der Frühling   spring
der Sommer   summer
der Herbst   autumn

der Winter   winter
im Herbst   in (the) autumn, fall
im Frühling   in (the) spring
jeden Sommer   every summer
jeden Winter   every winter
nächsten Winter   next winter
letzten Frühling   last spring
vorigen Herbst   last (*the previous*) autumn

The Year

das Jahr, -e   year, years
jedes Jahr   every year
jährlich   yearly, annual
Jahres-   yearly, annual (*used in compound words, such as* Jahresbericht, *"annual report."*)

das Jahrhundert, -e   century, centuries
das Jahrzehnt, -e   decade, decades
das Jahrtausend, -e   millenium, millenia

Telling Time

Wieviel Uhr ist es? *or* Wie spät ist es?	What time is it?
Es ist 9.34 Uhr. (neun Uhr vierunddreißig.)	It is 9:34.
Es ist 8.15 Uhr. (acht Uhr fünfzehn./Viertel nach acht./Viertel neun.*)	It is 8:15./a quarter past eight.
Es ist 7.30 Uhr. (sieben Uhr dreißig./halb acht.*).	It is 7:30.
Es ist 6.45 Uhr. (sechs Uhr fünfundvierzig./Viertel vor sieben./Dreiviertel sieben.*)	It is 6:45./a quarter to seven.

*Note: Telling time at a quarter, half, and three-quarters *before* the next hour are expressions commonly heard in the South. However, they are becoming common in other parts of the German-speaking world as well.

Telling time according to a 24-hour clock is the method used for all official time expressions, such as those found in railroad stations, airports, radio broadcasts, television programs, and university schedules. However, the 24-hour method of telling time does not use expressions such as *Viertel nach* or *Dreiviertel vor*. Only the hour followed by the minutes is used.

Die Zeit beim Gongschlag ist 21.10 Uhr (einundzwanzig Uhr zehn).	The time at the tone is 9:10 p.m.
Die Vorlesung beginnt um 13.30 Uhr (dreizehn Uhr dreißig).	The lecture begins at 1:30 p.m.

Dates

Heute is Freitag, der fünfte Mai neunzehnhundertvierundachtzig (der 5. Mai 1984).
Today is Friday, the fifth of May 1984.

Heute haben wir Freitag, den fünften Mai 1984 (den 5. Mai 1984).
Today is the fifth of May 1984.

Mein Geburtstag ist am siebenundzwanigsten April (am 27. April).
My birthday is on the twenty-seventh of April.

Mein vierzigster Geburtstag war am Freitag, dem 27. April 1984.
My 40th birthday was on Friday, April 27, 1984.

Other Time Expressions

ab und zu now and then
damalig- at that time (*adjective*)
damals at that time (*in the past*)
dann then
gelegentlich occasionally
gestern yesterday
gestern abend yesterday evening
gestrig- yesterday (*adjective*)
häufig frequently
heute today
heute früh this morning
heute abend this evening, tonight
heute nacht last night
heutig- today (*adjective*)
immer always
jetzig- now, the present (*adjective*)
jetzt now
manchmal sometimes
morgen tomorrow
morgen früh tomorrow morning

morgig- tomorrow (*adjective*)
nie never
oft often
selten rarely
übermorgen the day after tomorrow
vorgestern the day before yesterday
das Mal, -e time, times (*point in time*)
die Zeit, -en time, times (*span of time*)
einmal (ig-) once (one time)
zweimal (ig-) twice (two times)
dreimal (ig-) three times
zehnmal ten times
hundertvierzigmal 140 times
das erste Mal the first time
zum ersten Mal for the first time
das zehnte Mal the tenth time
zum zehnten Mal for the tenth time
das letzte Mal the last time
zum letzten Mal for the last time
das nächste Mal the next time

33. Vocabulary Lists

Territorial Divisions

das Land, Länder land, country, rural area
die Stadt, Städte city, urban area
die Hauptstadt, Hauptstädte capital
die Gemeinde, -n community
der Bezirk, -e district
der Bund, Bünde federation

das Bundesland, Bundesländer state (*in Germany and Austria*)
der Bundesstaat, -en state (in the USA)
der (Land) Kreis, -e "(land) circle" (*equivalent of American county*)

The German-Speaking Countries

die Bundesrepublik Deutschland (Westdeutschland) the Federal Republic of Germany (West Germany)
die Deutsche Demokratische Republik (Ostdeutschland) the German Democratic Republic (East Germany)
das Fürstentum Liechtenstein the Principality of Liechtenstein

die Republik Österreich (Österreich) the Republic of Austria (Austria)
die Schweizerische Eidgenossenschaft (die Schweiz) the Swiss Confederation (Switzerland)

Commonly Used Words and Phrases

Everyday Greetings and Expressions

Grüß Gott! Hello! (*in the South*)
Gute Nacht! Good night!
Guten Abend! Good evening!
Guten Tag! Hello! Good day!
Servus! Hello! (*in the South; also* "Good-bye")
Ade! Good-bye! (*in the South*)
Auf Wiederhören! Good-bye! (*on radio or telephone*)
Auf Wiederschauen! Good-bye!
Auf Wiedersehen! Good-bye!
Tschüß Good-bye! (*colloquial*)
Auf Ihr/dein/euer Wohl! To your health!
Pros(i)t! Cheers!
Zum Wohl! To your health!
Guten Appetit! "Bon appetit!"
Laß es Ihnen/dir/euch schmecken! "Bon appetit!" (*formal*)

Mahlzeit! "Bon appetit!" (*colloquial*)
Ich (wir) gratuliere(n)! Congratulations!
Kommen Sie/komm/kommt gut nach Hause! Arrive home safely!
Gute Fahrt/Reise! Have a pleasant trip! "Bon voyage!"
Viel Glück! Good luck!
Viel Erfolg! Good luck! Hope you're successful!
Hals- und Beinbruch! Break a leg!
Toi, toi, toi! Good luck!
Angenehme Ruhe! Sleep well!
Viel Vergnügen! Have a good time!
Achtung! (Auf die Plätze!) Ready! (On your mark!)
Fertig! Get set!
Los! Go!

Responses

Ja Yes
Nein No
Vielleicht Perhaps
Doch! Yes, definitely (*contradicts negatives*)
Natürlich! ⎫
Selbstverständlich! ⎬ Of course!
Sicher! ⎪
Freilich! ⎭
Das kommt darauf an. That depends.
Das geht Sie/dich/euch nichts an! That is none of your business!
Bitte? What was that? Please repeat.
Bitte ⎫
Bitte sehr ⎬ Please. Here you are. You're welcome.
Bitte schön ⎭
Quatsch! ⎫
Unsinn! ⎬ Nonsense!
Blödsinn! ⎭
Gleichfalls ⎫
Ihnen/dir/euch auch ⎬ Same to you

Na und? So what?
Ach ja? Oh, really?
Also! So! Now then! As I was saying...
Aufpassen! Be careful! Watch out!
Vorsicht! Be careful!
Meinetwegen As far as I'm concerned
Entschuldigung! Excuse me! (*to get someone's attention*)
Verzeihung! Pardon me! (*to ask forgiveness*)
Danke ⎫
Vielen Dank ⎬ Thank you
Danke vielmals ⎭
Wieso? How come?
Also gut! All right, it's decided!
(Aber) Trotzdem... (But) Just the same...
Ruhe! Silence! Be quiet!
Hilfe! Help!

The Family

die Familie, -n family

die (Ur) (Groß) Eltern (great) (grand) parents
der (Ehe) Mann, (Ehe) Männer husband
die (Ehe) Frau, -en wife
der Großvater grandfather
die Großmutter, Großmütter grandmother
der Urgroßvater, Urgroßväter great grandfather
die Urgroßmutter, Urgroßmütter great grandmother
der Onkel, - uncle
die Tante, -n aunt
das Kind, -er child
der Sohn, Söhne son

die Tochter, Töchter daughter
der Bruder, Brüder brother
die Schwester, -n sister
der Schwager, -* brother-in-law
die Schwägerin, -nen* sister-in-law
der Vetter, -n cousin (*masc.*)
die Kusine, -n cousin (*fem.*)
der Neffe, -n nephew
die Nichte, -n niece
der (Ur) Enkel, - (great) grandson
die (Ur) Enkelin, -nen (great) granddaughter
der Verwandte, -n relative (*masc.*) (ein Verwandter)
die Verwandte, -n relative (*fem.*)

*Note: The prefix *Schwieger-* means "-in-law" for other relatives, for example *Schwiegersohn*, "son-in-law."

Characteristics (*Nouns*)

die Eigenschaft, -en   characteristic

das Alter   age
die Armut   poverty
die Aufregung   excitement
das Böse   the bad, the evil
die Breite, -n   width
die Dummheit, -en   stupidity
die Entfernung, -n   distance
das Falsche   the false
die Faulheit   laziness
die Feindseligkeit   hostility
der Fleiß   industriousness
die Freundschaft   friendship
der Frieden   peace
das Gewicht, -e   weight
die Größe, -n   size
die Güte   goodness, quality
das Gute   the good

die Härte, -n   hardness
die Höhe   height
die Jugend   youth
die Länge, -n   length
die Langeweile   boredom
die Lüge, -n   lie
der Reichtum   wealth
das Richtige   the correct
die Schwäche, -n   weakness
die Schwierigkeit, -en   difficulty
die Stärke, -n   strength
die Schönheit, -en   beauty
die Spannung   tension
die Treue   faithfulness
der Wahnsinn   insanity
die Wahrheit   truth
die Weisheit   wisdom

Characteristics (*Adjectives*)

alt   old
aufgeregt   excited
aufregend   exciting, stirring
billig   cheap
böse   angry, bad, evil
doof   stupid (*colloquial*)
dumm   dumb, stupid
einfach   easy
falsch   false, wrong
faul   lazy
feindlich   hostile
fleißig   industrious, hard-working
friedlich   peace-loving
freundlich   friendly
früh   early
gespannt   eager, thrilled, excited
gut   good
hart   hard
häßlich   ugly
intelligent   intelligent
interessant   interesting
jung   young
klug   intelligent, smart
langweilig   boring
laut   loud, noisy
leicht   light, easy
leise   quiet
lieb   dear, nice
nah   near
nett   nice

neu   new
preiswert   inexpensive
pünktlich   on time, punctual
rauh   rough
rechtzeitig   in time
reich   rich
roh   raw
ruhig   peaceful, quiet
sanft   smooth, soft (*surface*)
schlecht   bad
schlimm   bad, unfortunate
schön   fine, beautiful, nice, good
schlau   clever
schwer   heavy
schwierig   difficult
spannend   exciting, suspenseful, absorbing
spät   late
teuer   expensive
treu   faithful
uralt   ancient, very old
verrückt   crazy, insane
wahnsinnig   insane
wahr   true
wild   wild
weich   soft (*texture*)
weise   wise
weit   far
zeitig   very early, ahead of time

Color

die Farbe, -n color

blau blue
braun brown
gelb yellow
grün green
grau gray
rot red

schwarz black
weiß white
dunkel dark
grell bright, loud (*color*)
hell light

Size

die Größe, -n size

breit wide
dick fat, thick
dünn thin
eng narrow
groß big, great, large, tall (*persons*)
hoch high, tall (*objects*)
klein small, little
lang long

kurz short
niedrig low
riesig giant
schwach weak
stark strong
tief deep
winzig tiny

The Weather (*Nouns*)

das Wetter weather

die Bewölkung cloudiness, overcast conditions
der Dunst haze
die Feuchtigkeit humidity
der Gefrierpunkt the freezing point
der Grad (*Celsius*) degree (*Celsius*)
der Hagel hail
die Hitze heat

die Kälte cold
der Nebel fog
der Regen rain
der Schnee snow
der Siedepunkt the boiling point
die Temperatur, -en temperature
die Wärme warmth
die Wolke, -n cloud

The Weather (*Adjectives*)

bewölkt cloudy
dunstig hazy
feucht humid
frisch fresh, brisk
heiß hot
heiter bright and sunny
kalt cold
klar clear

kühl cool
nebelig foggy
regnerisch rainy
schwül muggy
trüb hazy, foggy, overcast
warm warm
wolkig cloudy

Everyday Objects

der Gegenstand, Gegenstände object

der Bericht, -e report
der Bleistift, -e pencil
der Bleistiftspitzer, - pencil sharpener
der Brief, -e letter *(correspondence)*
die Briefmarke, -n postage stamp
das Buch, Bücher book
der Buchstabe, -n letter of the alphabet
das Heft, -e notebook, notepad
die Kreide chalk
der Kugelschreiber, - ballpoint pen
der Kuli, -s ballpoint pen *(colloquial)*
die Mine, -n ballpoint pen refill cartridge
das Papier, -e paper *(the material or documents)*
der Radiergummi, -s eraser
das Referat, -e (term) paper
der Schwamm, Schwamme blackboard eraser, sponge
der Stempel, - rubber stamp
die Tinte ink
der Umschlag, Umschlage envelope

The House

das Haus, Häuser house

der Ausgang exit
das Badezimmer, - bath
der Eingang entrance
das Eßzimmer, - dining room
der Fußboden, Fußböden floor of a room
der Gang, Gänge corridor, aisle
die Garage, - garage
der Garten, Gärten garden, yard
die Küche, -n kitchen
die Mauer, -n wall *(freestanding)*
der Rasen lawn
das Schlafzimmer, - bedroom
das Schloß, Schlösser lock
der Schlüssel, - key
die Tür, -en door
das Wohnzimmer, - living room

The Room

das Zimmer, - room

das (Bücher) Regal, -e bookcase
die Bude, -n very small room
die Decke, -n ceiling, blanket
die Ecke, -n corner
das Fenster, - window
die Gardine, -n curtain
der Hocker, - stool
die Lampe, -n lamp
das Möbel, - furniture
der Raum, Räume large room
der Regalboden, Regalböden shelf
der Schrank, Schränke cupboard, cabinet, closet
der Schreibtisch, -e desk
das Sofa, -s sofa
der Spiegel, - mirror
die Stube, -n small room
der Stuhl, Stühle chair
der Teppich, -e rug
die Uhr, -en clock, watch, timepiece
der Vorhang, Vorhänge drape, curtain
die Wand, Wände wall *(inside a building)*

The Bed

das Bett, -en bed

der Bettlaken, - sheet
das Bettuch, Bettücher sheet
die Decke, -en blanket
das Kissen, - pillow
die Matraze, -n mattress

The Table

der Tisch, -e table

das Besteck silverware
der Essig vinegar
die Gabel, -n fork
das Geschirr plates, cup, saucers, pots, pans, etc.
das Glas, Gläser glass
der Krug, Krüge pitcher, beer mug ("Stein")
der Löffel, - spoon
das Messer, - knife

das Öl oil
das Pfeffer pepper
die Platte, -n platter
das Salz salt
die Serviette, -n napkin
die Tasse, -n cup
der Teller, - plate
die Tischdecke, -n table cloth
die Untertasse, -n saucer
der Zucker sugar

Beverages

das Getränk, -e beverage

das Bier beer
der Kaffee coffee
der Kakao cocoa
die Limonade, -n soft drink
die Milch milk

der Most cider
der Saft, Säfte juice
der Tee tea
das Wasser water
der Wein wine

Meat

das Fleisch meat

der Braten, - roast
das Hammelfleisch mutton
das Kotlett, -en cutlet, chop
das Kalbfleisch veal
das Lammfleisch lamb
das Rindfleisch beef

der Schinken, - ham
das Schnitzel, - cutlet, tenderloin
das Schweinefleisch pork
der Speck bacon
die Wurst, Würste sausage

Poultry

das Geflügel poultry, fowl

die Ente, -n duck
die Gans, Gänse goose
das Huhn, Hühner chicken

der Pute, -n turkey
der Truthahn, Truthähne turkey

Fish

der Fisch, -e fish

der Aal, -e eel
die Forelle, -n trout
der Kabeljau cod

der Karpfen, - carp
der Lachs, -e salmon

Vegetables

das Gemüse vegetables

der Blumenkohl cauliflower
die Bohne, -n bean
die Erbse, -n pea
die Gurke, -n cucumber, pickle
die Karotte, -n carrot
die Kartoffel, -n potato
der Knoblauch garlic
der Kohl cabbage
der Kürbis, -e squash, pumpkin

die Linse, -n lentil
die Möhre, -n carrot
die Olive, -n olive
der Rettich, -e raddish
der Rosenkohl brussels sprouts
der Salat lettuce (*also*, salad)
der Schnittlauch chives
die Tomate, -n tomato
die Zwiebel, -n onion

Grain

das Getreide cereal grains

die Gerste barley
der Mais corn
der Reis rice

die Rogge rye
der Weizen wheat

Fruits

das Obst fruits

die Ananas, - pineapple
der Apfel, Äpfel apple
die Aprikose, -n apricot
die Banane, -n banana
die Birne, -n pear
die Dattel, -n date
die Erdbeere, -n strawberry
die Feige, -n fig
die Himbeere, -n raspberry
die Johannisbeere, -n currant

die Kirsche, -n cherry
die Limone, -n lime
die Melone, -n melon
die Orange, -n orange
der Pfirsich, -e peach
die Pflaume, -n plum
die Preiselbeere, -n cranberry
die Stachelbeere, -n gooseberry
die Traube, -n grape
die Zitrone, -n lemon

Food and Meals

die Mahlzeit, -en meal time
die Nahrung food, nourishment

das Abendbrot supper
das Abendessen dinner
die Beilage, -n side dish, side order
das Brot bread
das Brötchen, - roll
die Butter butter
das Ei, -er egg
der Eintopf stew
das Eis ice, ice cream
die Erfrischung refreshment
das Essen food
das Frühstück breakfast
das Gebäck pastry, baked goods
das Gericht, -e meal, "dish"
das Hauptgericht, -e main dish

der Honig honey
der Imbiß snack
der Käse cheese
der Kuchen, - cake
die Marmelade marmelade
das Mittagessen lunch
der Nachtisch dessert
der Salat, -e salad
der Senf mustard
die Soße, -n sauce
die Speise, -n meal, food
die Speisekarte, -n menu
die Suppe, -n soup
die Torte, -n pie, pastry

Animals

das Tier, -e animal

    der Bär, -en bear
    der Bulle, -n breed bull
    das Eichhörnchen, - squirrel
    der Fuchs, Füchse fox
    der Hase, -n hare
    der Hengst, -e stallion
    der Hund, -e dog
    die Hundin, -nen female dog
    das Kalb, Kälber calf
    das Kaninchen, - rabbit
    die Katze, -n cat
    der Kater, - male cat, tom cat

    die Kuh, Kühe cow
    das Kätzchen, - kitten
    der Löwe, -n lion
    die Maus, Mäuse mouse
    das Pferd, -e horse
    die Ratte, -n rat
    die Schildkröte, -n turtle
    die Schlange, -n snake
    der Stier, -e bull
    die Stute, -n mare
    der Wolf, Wölfe wolf
    der Wurm, Würmer worm

Birds

der Vogel, Vögel bird

    der Adler, - eagle
    der Eichelhäher, - blue jay
    die Elster, -n magpie
    der Hahn, Hähne rooster, cock
    die Henne, -n hen
    das Kücken, - chick

    der Papagei, -en parrot
    die Schwalbe, -n swallow
    der Sittich, -e parakeet
    der Spatz, -en sparrow
    der Specht, -e woodpecker
    die Taube, -n pigeon, dove

Insects

das Insekt, -e insect

    die Ameise, -n ant
    die Biene, -n bee
    die Fliege, -n fly
    der Floh, Flöhe flea
    die Heuschrecke, -n grasshopper

    die Motte, -n moth
    die Mücke, -n mosquito
    der Schmetterling, -e butterfly
    die Spinne, -n spider

Trees

der Baum, Bäume tree

    der Ahorn maple
    der Ast, Äste (large) branch
    der (Baum)Stamm, (Baum)Stämme trunk, log
    die Eiche, -n oak
    die Rinde bark
    die Kastanie, -n chestnut
    die Kiefer, -n spruce

    die Linde, -n linden
    die Palme, -n palm
    die Papel, -n poplar
    die Tanne, -n fir, spruce
    der (Wal)Nußbaum, (Wal)Nußbäume walnut
    die Wurzel, -n root
    der Zweig, -e (small) branch, twig

Plants and Flowers

die Pflanze, -n plant

die Blume, -n flower
die Blumenzwiebel, -n flower bulb
die Blüte, -n blossom
das Blatt, Blätter leaf
das Blütenblatt, Blütenblätter petal
der Flieder lilac
die Gänseblume, -n daisy
das Gras grass

die Lilie, -n lily
der Löwenzahn dandelion
das Maiglöckchen, - lily of the valley
die Nelke, -n carnation
die Rose, -n rose
die Tulpe, -n tulip
das Veilchen, - violet

The Earth

die Erde earth, soil, ground

die Atmosphäre atmosphere
der Bach, Bäche stream
der Berg, -e mountain
der Boden, Böden floor, bottom, ground
die Bucht, -en bay
das Feld, -er field
der Fluß, Flüsse river
das Gebirge, - mountain range
der Golf, -e gulf
die Halbinsel, -n peninsula
der Himmel sky
die Höhle, -n cave
der Hügel, - hill
die Insel, -n island
das Kap, -s cape

der Kontinent, -en continent
die Küste, -n coast
die Landschaft landscape, scenery
die Luft air
das Meer, -e sea, ocean
der See, -n lake
der Strand, Strände beach
der Sumpf, Sümpfe swamp, marsh
das Tal, Täler valley
der Teich, -e pond
das Ufer, - shore
der Wald, Wälder forest
der Weiher, - fish pond
die Wiese, -n meadow
die Wüste, -n desert

The City

die Stadt, Städte city

die Großstadt, Großstädte city *(over 100,000 population)*
die Kleinstadt, Kleinstädte town *(under 100,000 population)*
die Allee, -n avenue
die Ampel, -n traffic light
die Bank, Bänke bench
die Bank, -en bank
die Bibliothek, -en library
der Bürgersteig, -e sidewalk
der Dom, -e cathedral
das Dorf, Dörfer village
die Fabrik, -en factory
der Friedhof, Friedhöfe cemetery
die Gasse, -n alley (street, *in Austria*)
der Gehsteig, -e sidewalk
die Gemeinde, -n community, municipality

der Hafen, Häfen port, harbor
das Kino, -s movie theater
die Kirche, -n church
das Krankenhaus, Krankenhäuser hospital
das Museum, Museen museum
der Park, -s park
der Pfad, -e path
der Platz, Plätze square
das Rathaus, Rathäuser city hall
die Rennbahn, -en race track
das Schild, -er traffic sign
das Stadion, Stadien stadium
die Straße, -n street
das Theater, - theater
der Weg, -e way

Shopping

das Geschäft, -e business, store
der Laden, Läden shop, store

    die Apotheke, -n pharmacy, drugstore
    die Bäckerei, -en bakery
    die Bar, -s cocktail lounge
    die Buchhandlung, -en bookstore
    das Cafe, -s cafe
    die Drogerie, -n drugstore (without drugs)
    die Einkaufstasche, -n shopping bag
    die Gaststätte, -n restaurant
    das Kaufhaus, Kaufhäuser department store
    die Kneipe, -n bar
    die Konditorei, -en pastry shop
    der Markt, Märkte market
    die Metzgerei, -en butcher shop
    das Restaurant, -s restaurant
    die Reinigung dry cleaning
    der Supermarkt, Supermärkte supermarket
    die Tüte, -n paper bag
    die Wäscherei, -en laundry

Transportation

der Verkehr traffic

    die Ausfahrt, -en exit
    das Auto, -s car
    die Autobahn, -en freeway
    das Autobahnkreuz, -e freeway interchange
    das Boot, -e boat
    der Bus, -e bus
    der Dampfer, - steamer
    die Einfahrt, -en entrance
    die (Eisen)Bahn, -en railway
    das Fahrrad, Fahrräder bicycle
    das Fahrzeug, -e vehicle
    der Flughafen, -häfen airport
    das Flugzeug, -e airplane
    der Fußänger, - pedestrian
    die Fußängerzone, -n pedestrian mall
    das Kreuz, -e cross, crossing
    die Kreuzung, -en crossing, junction
    der Lastwagen, - truck
    der LKW, -s* truck
    die Maschine, -n (commercial) airplane
    das Motorrad, Motorräder motorcycle
    der PKW, -s* passenger vehicle, car
    die S-Bahn rapid transit
    das Schiff, -e ship
    das Segelboot, -e sailboat
    die Spur, -en traffic land
    die Straßenbahn, -en streetcar, tram
    das Taxi, -s taxi
    die U-Bahn underground, subway
    der Verkehrsstau, -s traffic jam
    der Wagen, - car
    die Zufahrt, -en approach

*Note: LKW = *Lastkraftwagen*, PKW = *Personenkraftwagen*

Travel

die Reise, -n trip, journey, travel

die Abfahrt, -en departure
die Ankunft, Ankünfte arrival
der Aufzug, Aufzüge elevator
der Bahnhof, -höfe railroad station
der Bahnsteig, -e platform
die Fahrkarte, -n ticket
die Fahrt, -en trip, drive
der Fahrplan, Fahrpläne travel schedule, time table
der Fensterplatz, Fensterplätze window seat
der Gangplatz, Gangplätze aisle seat
das Gepäck baggage, luggage
der Gepäckträger, - porter
das Gleis, -e track

das Hotel, -s hotel
die Jugendherberge, -n youth hostel
der Koffer, - suitcase
der Liegewagen, - sleeping car
die Lokomotive, -n locomotive
die Reisetasche, -n travel bag
der Schaffner, - conductor
der Schalter, - (ticket) window
der Schlafwagen, - sleeping car, pullman
die Sehenswürdigkeit, -en sight *(something worth seeing)*
der (Sitz)Platz, (Sitz)Plätze seat
der Speisewagen, - dining car
der Zug, Züge train

The Human Body

der Körper, - body

die Ader, -n artery
der Arm, -e arm
das Auge, -n eye
die Backe, -n cheek
die Bandscheibe, -n vertebra
der Bauch, Bäuche abdomen, belly
die Bauchspeicheldrüse, -n pancreas
das Bein, -e leg
die Blase, -n bladder
die Brust, Brüste chest, breast
die Drüse, -n gland
der Finger, - finger
der Fuß, Füsse foot
das Fußgelenk, -e ankle
das Gehirn brain
das Haar, -e hair
der Hals, Hälse neck
die Hand, Hände hand
das Handgelenk, -e wrist
die Haut, Häute skin
das Herz, -en heart
der Kiefer, - jaw
das Kinn, -e chin
das Knie, - knee

der Knochen, - bone
der Kopf, Köpfe head
die Kopfhaut scalp
der Kreislauf circulatory system
die Leber, -n liver
die Lippe, -n lip
die Lunge, -n lung
der Magen, Mägen stomach
die Milz, -en spleen
der Nagel, Nägel nail
der Mund, Münder mouth
die Nase, -n nose
der Nerv, -en nerve
die Niere, -n kidney
das Ohr, -en ear
der Rücken, - back
die Schulter, -n shoulder
die Stirn, -en forehead
die Vene, -n vein
die Wange, -n cheek
die Wirbelsäule, -n spinal column
der Zahn, Zähne teeth
die Zehe, -n toe
die Zunge, -n tongue

Clothing

die Kleidung clothing

die Armbanduhr, -en wristwatch
der Ärmel, - sleeve
das Badetuch, Badetücher bath towel
die Bluse, -n blouse
die Handtasche, -n handbag, purse
das Handtuch, Handtücher towel
das Hemd, -en shirt
die Hose, -n pair of trousers
das Kleid, -er dress
der Kragen, - collar
die Krawatte, -n tie
der Rock, Röcke skirt

der Schuh, -e shoe
die Schürze, -n apron
die Socke, -n sock
der Stiefel, - boot
der Strumpf, Strümpfe stockings
die Tasche, -n bag, sack, pocket, purse, pouch
das Taschentuch, Taschentücher handkerchief
die Taschenuhr, -en pocket watch
die Unterwäsche underwear
die Wäsche laundry

Professions

die Arbeit work

der Beruf, -e profession
der (Rechts)Anwalt, (Rechts)Anwälte } lawyer
die (Rechts)Anwältin. -nen
der Architekt, -en } architect
die Architektin, -nen
der Arzt, Ärzte } physician
die Ärztin, -nen
die (Erz)Bischof, (Erz)Bischöfe (arch)bishop
der Fotograf, -en } photographer
die Fotografin, -nen
der Geistliche, -n clergyman
der Imam, -e *(islamisch)* imam *(Islamic)*
der Kardinal, Kardinäle cardinal
der Lehrer, - } teacher
die Lehrerin, -nen
der Matrose, -n sailor
der Musiker, - } musician
die Musikerin, -nen

der Papist, Päpste pope
der Pfarrer, - *(evangelisch)* minister *(Protestant, Lutheran)*
der Pilot, -en } pilot
die Pilotin, -nen
der Polizist, -en } police officer
die Polizistin, -nen
der Priester, - *(katholisch)* priest *(Catholic)*
der Rabbiner, - *(jüdisch)* rabbi *(Jewish)*
der Schauspieler, - } actor
die Schauspielerin, -nen
die Schreibkraft, Schreibkräfte file clerk
der Sekretär, -en } secretary
die Sekretärin, -nen
der Soldat, -en soldier
der Zahnarzt, Zahnärzte } dentist
die Zahnärztin, -nen

Education

der Abschluß   degree, completion of studies
die Abschlußklausur, -en   final examination
die Ausbildung   professional training
die Bildung   learning, culture, education
das Diplom, -e   diploma *(in natural sciences)*
der Doktor(grad)   doctorate
die Erziehung   education, teaching
das Examen, -   examination
die Hochschule, -n   university
die Klausur, -en   (in-class) test
der Magister(grad)   masters
die Prüfung, -en   test, examination
die Schule, -n   school
der Schüler, -   pupil *(primary or secondary)*
die Schülerin, -nen
der Student, -en   student *(university only)*
die Studentin, -nen
das Studium, Studien   academic study
der Stundenplan, Stundenpläne   schedule, time table
die Universität, -en   university
das Vorlesungsverzeichnis, -se   university catalogue

Academic Subjects

das Fach, Fächer   subject
das Hauptfach, Hauptfächer   major subject
das Nebenfach, Nebenfächer   minor subject

(die) Amerikanistik   American studies
(die) Anglistik   English language and literature
(die) Biologie   biology
(die) Erziehungswissenschaften   education
(die) Fremdsprache, -n   foreign language
(die) Geisteswissenschaft, -en   humanities
(die) Germanistik   German language and literature
(die) Geschichte   history
(die) Informatik   information or computer sciences
(die) Ingenieurwissenschaften   engineering
(die) Mathematik   mathematics
(die) Naturwissenschaft, -en   natural sciences
(die) Philosophie   philosophy
(die) Physik   physics
(die) Romanistik   Romance languages and literatures
(die) Theologie   theology
(die) Wirtschaftswissenschaften   economics

Titles

der Titel, -   titel

die Anrede, -n   forms of address
(der) Herr, -en   Mr., Lord, sir
(die) Frau, -en   Mrs., Ms., woman, lady
der Präsident, -en   president
Herr Präsident   Mr. President
die Präsidentin, -nen   president
Frau Präsidentin   Madame President
der Professor, -en ⎫
die Professorin, -nen ⎬ professor
Herr Professor   Professor *(man)*
Frau Professor   Professor *(woman)*
der Doktor, -en   Ph.D., Doctor of philosophy. *(any doctorate)*
Herr Doktor   Doctor *(man)*
Frau Doktor   Doctor *(woman)*
der Minister, - ⎫
die Ministerin, -nen ⎬ minister (of state)
Herr Minister   Mister Minister
Frau Ministerin   Madame Minister

Units of Measurement

das Maß, Masse measurement

der *or* **das Liter, -** liter
das *or* **der Meter, -** meter
das Gramm, - gram
das Kilo(gramm), - kilo(gram)
das Pfund, - one-half kilogram, 500 grams

das *or* **der Kilometer, -** kilometer
das Hektar, - hectare
der Zoll, - inch
der Fuß, - foot
die Gallone, -n gallon
die Tonne, -n (metric) ton

Geometry

die Geometrie geometry

der Winkel, - angle
der rechte Winkel, - right angle
das Rechteck, -e square
das Viereck, -e rectangle
das Dreieck, - triangle
der Kreis, -e circle
der Halbkreis, -e semicircle
der Durchmesser diameter
der Radius/Halbmesser radius

die Linie, -n line
der Rhombus rhombus
der Würfel, - cube
die Kegel, -n cone
die Kugel, -n sphere
die Halbkugel, -n hemisphere
die Pyramide, -n pyramid
das Prisma, Prismen prism

Chemistry

die Chemie chemistry

das Element, -e element
die Flüssigkeit, -en liquid
das Gas, -e gas
das Metall, -e metal
das Blei lead
das Eisen iron
das Gold gold

der Kohlenstoff carbon
das Kupfer copper
der Sauerstoff oxygen
das Silber silver
der Stickstoff nitrogen
der Wasserstoff hydrogen
das Zinn tin

Materials

der Backstein brick
die Baumwolle cotton
der Beton concrete
der Gips plaster
das Glas glass
der Gummi rubber
das Holz wood
der Kalkstein limestone
die Keramik ceramic
der Kunststoff plastic

der Marmor marble
das Metall metal
das Plastik plastic
die Seide silk
der Stahl steel
der Stein stone
der Stoff, -e material, fabric
der Stuk stucco
die Wolle wool
der Ziegel tile

Holidays and Holiday Greetings

der Feiertag, -e holiday
das Fest, -e festival
die Feier, -n celebration
die Ferien (plural) holidays, vacation
der Urlaub vacation
Frohe Festtage! Happy Holidays!
(das) Weihnachten* Christmas
(der) Heilige Abend Christmas Eve
Frohe Weihnachten! Merry Christmas!
Fröhliche Weihnachten!
(das) Neujahr New Year's Day
Gutes Neues Jahr! Happy New Year!
(der) Sylvester New Year's Eve
(das) Ostern* Easter
Frohe Ostern! Happy Easter!
(das) Pfingsten* Pentecost
(der) Heilige(r) Sankt Nikolaus Saint Nicholas' Day *(December 6)*
(die) Heilige(n) Drei Könige Epiphany *(January 6)*
(der) Rosenmontag Monday before Ash Wednesday
(der) Faschingsdienstag Tuesday before Ash Wednesday
(der) Aschermittwoch Ash Wednesday
(der) Gründonnerstag Holy Thursday
(der) Karfreitag Good Friday

*Note: *Weihnachten, Ostern,* and *Pfingsten* usually appear in the plural, as in *Frohe Weihnachten,* or in compounds, such as *Ostersonntag* ("Easter Sunday") or *Pfingstwoche* ("Week of Pentecost").

Abbreviations

die Abkürzung, -en abbreviation

AG Aktiengesellschaft (stock) corporation
Betr. Betreff/betrifft re, regarding
bzw. beziehungsweise or (respectively)
Fa. Firma _____ _____Company
Fam. Familie _____ (Mr. and Mrs.) _____ and family
Fr. Frau Mrs., Ms.
Frl. Fräulein Miss
GmbH Gesellschaft mit beschränkter Haftung (limited liability) corporation, Ltd.
Hr(n). Herr(n) Mr.
i. R. im Ruhestand retired
Nr. Nummer number, No.
PLZ Postleitzahl postal code, ZIP Code
usw. und so weiter and so on, etc.
vgl. vergleiche compare, cf.
z. B. zum Beispiel for example, e.g.
z. Z. zur Zeit at present

Index

ab-, 30
abbreviations, 115
academic subjects (vocabulary), 113
accusative case, 68, 69, 70-71, 85, 87, 88, 89, 93
active voice, 42
adjectives, 73-75, 76, 79, 82, 84, 103, 104
   case, 73-74, 79
   characteristics of, 73
   color (vocabulary), 104
   comparison of, 73, 74-75, 76
   demonstrative, 82
   gender, 73-74, 79
   irregular, 76
   number, 73-74, 79
   possessive, 84
   size (vocabulary), 104
   weather (vocabulary), 104
adverbs, 73, 74-75, 76-77
   comparison of, 74-75
   formation of, 73, 76
   irregular, 76-77
alphabet, 3, 65
am liebsten, 77
am . . . sten, 75, 76
an-, 30
anderthalb, 80
animals (vocabulary), 108
arbeiten, 9, 24
article, 63, 64-67, 78
   definite, 63, 64, 73, 74
   indefinite, 63, 73, 74, 78
   with geographical names, 64, 65, 101
auf-, 30
aus-, 30
auxiliary verbs, *see* verbs

-bar, 97
be-, 25, 32
bei-, 30
beverages (vocabulary), 106
birds (vocabulary), 108
bis, 28, 69
body (vocabulary), 111

capitalization, 64
case, 63, 67-68
   accusative, 68, 69, 70-71, 85, 87, 88, 89, 93
   dative, 68, 69-70, 70-71, 85, 87, 89, 93
   genitive, 68, 70, 74, 85, 87, 89, 93
   nominative, 67, 85, 87, 89, 93
characteristics (vocabulary), 103
chemistry (vocabulary), 114
-chen, 64
city, the (vocabulary), 101, 109
clauses:
   main, 94-95
   subordinate, 94, 95
clothing (vocabulary), 112
color (vocabulary), 104
commands, *see* imperative mood
consonants, 4-5
contractions, 72
countries, 65, 101

da(r)-, 85-86
das, 83
dates, 100
dative case, 68, 69-70, 70-71, 85, 87, 89, 93
days, 66, 98
dein/deine, 84, 92
demonstrative adjectives, 64, 82, 84
der/die/das, 63, 73-74, 82, 86, 89-90
dessen/deren, 89, 90
direct object, 68
du, 6, 34, 35, 85, 87
durch- (prefix), 25, 30
dürfen, 15, 22, 37

earth, the (vocabulary), 109
education (vocabulary), 113
-ei, 97
ein- (prefix), 30
ein/eine (indefinite article), 63, 73-74, 78
einhalb, 80
emp-, 25, 32
empfehlen, 44-46 (summary of forms)
ent-, 25, 32
er- (prefix), 25, 32

117

er (pronoun), 6, 85, 86
-er (suffix), 74, 75, 97
-erei, 65, 97
euer, 84, 85
exclamations, *see also* responses, 93, 101, 102

family (vocabulary), 102
fish (vocabulary), 106
"flavor" words, 93
flowers (vocabulary), *see* plants
food (vocabulary), 106-107
fractions, 80
fruits (vocabulary), 107
future tense, 16, 37, 42
future perfect tense, 23, 28, 42

ge-, 23-24
geben, 9-10, 37, 39
gehen, 37, 40
gender, 63
    of adjectives, 73-74
    of nouns, 64-67
    of pronouns, 64, 89
genitive case, 68, 70, 74, 85, 87, 89, 93
geographical names (vocabulary), *see also* territorial divisions, 65, 101
geometry (vocabulary), 114
gern, 77
grain (vocabulary), 107
greetings (vocabulary), 101, 115

haben, 12, 20, 26, 27, 28, 37, 40, 44, 46-48 (summary of forms), 56
halb, 80
Hälfte, 80
-heit, 65, 97
her-, 30
hin-, 30
holidays (vocabulary), 115
house, the (vocabulary), 105-106
hypothetical subjunctive, *see* subjunctive mood

ich, 6, 85, 87
-ie, 65, 97
-ieren, 25, 97
-ig, 97
ihr (pronoun), 6, 34, 35, 85, 87
ihr/ihre, 84, 92
Ihr/Ihre, 84
imperative mood, 34-35, 36
-in, 97

indicative mood, 7-33, 36
    compound tenses, 26-27, 28-29, 40
    simple tenses, 7-11, 12-13, 14-15, 16, 17-18, 19-20, 21-22
indirect discourse, *see* subjunctive mood
indirect object, 68
infinitive, 7, 15, 24, 25, 40
insects (vocabulary), 108
inseparable prefixes, 32-33
interrogatives, 11, 93
irregular verbs, 12-13, 14-15, 19-20, 21-22
-isch, 97

kein/keine, 74, 78, 92
-keit, 65, 97
kommen, 37, 44, 48-49 (summary of forms)
können, 14, 21, 37, 44, 50-51 (summary of forms)

-lein, 64
"let's . . .", 35
lieber, 77
-los, 97

machen, 8, 16, 17, 36, 37, 38, 39, 40, 44
man, 6, 12
materials (vocabulary), 114
meals (vocabulary), 107
measurement (vocabulary), 114
meat (vocabulary), 106
mein/meine, 84
mixed verbs, *see* verbs
modal verbs, *see* verbs
mögen, 15, 22, 37
months, 98
müssen, 14-15, 21

nach-, 30
negatives, 11, 91-92
nicht, 11, 91
nicht müssen, 21
nominative case, 67, 85, 87, 89, 93
nouns, 64-68, 92, 103, 104
    case, *see* case
    gender, 64-66
    number (plural), 63, 66-67
numbers, 78-81
    arithmetic, 81
    cardinal numbers, 78-79
    fractions, 80
    numerals, 78, 80
    ordinal numbers, 79-80

objects:
  direct, 68
  indirect, 68
  of prepositions, 68, 69-72
  of reflexive verbs, 88

passive voice:
  formation of, 41-42
  uses of, 41
  von, 43
past participle, 23-27, 41-42
  formation of, 23-25
  without **ge-,** 24-25
past perfect tense, 23, 28, 42
plants (vocabulary), 109
pluperfect, see past perfect tense
plural, see nouns
possession:
  adjectives, 84
  genitive, 68
  pronouns, 84
poultry (vocabulary), 106
prefixes, 25, 30-33
  inseparable, 32-33
  separable, 30-31, 33
prepositions, 69-72, 85-86
  contractions, 72
  with accusative, 68, 69, 70-71, 72
  with dative, 68, 69-70, 70-71, 72
  with genitive, 68, 70
present tense, 7-11, 12-13, 14-15, 34, 35, 36
present perfect tense, 23, 26-27, 40, 42, 44-45
preterite tense, 17-18, 19-20, 21-22, 36, 41, 44-45
principle parts of verbs, 55-60
professions (vocabulary), 112
pronouns, 6, 64, 67, 91
  demonstrative, 82, 83
  gender, 64, 89
  interrogative, 93
  object, 85-86
  personal, 6, 85
  possessive, 84
  reflexive, 87-88
  relative, 89-90
  subject, 6, 64, 85
pronunciation: 3-5
  consonants, 4-5
  umlaut, 3
  vowels, 3-4
punctuation, 5

questions, see interrogatives

reflexives, 87
  pronouns, 87-88
  verbs, 87-88
relative pronouns, 89-90
responses (vocabulary), 102

-schaft, 65
seasons, 99
sehen, 10, 19-20, 38, 41, 42
sein (verb), 12, 20, 27, 28, 35, 37, 39, 40, 42, 44, 51-52 (summary of forms), 55, 59
sein/seine (adjective), 84, 92
sentence rules, 94-96
separable prefixes, 30-31, 33
shopping (vocabulary), 110
sich, 87-88
sie, 6, 85, 86
Sie, 6, 12, 34, 35, 87
simple past, see preterite tense
size (vocabulary), 104
sollen, 14, 21, 37
sondern, 92
stem, 7, 8-9, 9-10, 21, 22, 34, 36, 37, 38
stem-vowel changes, 9-10, 44
strong verbs, 19-20, 25, 55-58
subject, 6, 67
subjunctive mood, 36
  formation of, 36-39, 40, 42
  hypothetical subjunctive, 36-38
  indirect discourse, 38-39
  tenses of, 36, 39, 40, 42
  uses of, 36, 38, 40
suchen, 44, 52-54 (summary of forms)
suffixes, 97

tenses, see individual tenses
territorial divisions (vocabulary), 101
time, 96, 98-100
titles (vocabulary), 113
tragen, 10, 39
transportation (vocabulary), 110
travel (vocabulary), 111
trees (vocabulary), 108
-tum, 97

um-, 25
units of measurement (vocabulary), 114
-ung, 65, 97
unser, 84
unter-, 25

vegetables (vocabulary), 107
ver-, 32
verbs:
   auxiliary, 26-27, 28
   irregular, 12-13, 14-15, 19-20
   mixed verbs, 22
   modal, 14-15, 16, 21-22, 26-27, 40, 44, 50-51
   principal parts, 55-60
   reflexive, 87-88
   stem-vowel change, 9-10, 44, 54
   strong, 19-20, 25, 55-58
   summary of forms, 44-60
   weak, 17-18, 23-25, 59-60
vocabulary lists, 101-115
von, 43
vor-, 30
vowels, 3-4

weak verbs, 17-18, 23-25, 59-60
weather (vocabulary), 104
wer, 93
werden, 13, 16, 20, 28, 37, 41, 42, 44, 54-55 (summary of forms)
wir, 6, 35, 85, 87
wissen, 13, 22, 37
wohl, 29
wollen, 14, 22, 37
wo(r)-, 86
worden, 42
word order:
   expressions of manner, 96
   expressions of place, 96
   expressions of time, 96
   verbs, 94-95
würde, 37, 45, 47, 49, 51, 53, 54, 55

zer-, 33
zu-, 30
zurück-, 30

Verb Index

This verb index will enable you to compare hundreds of commonly used verbs to the book's numerous verb tables. Each group of regular or irregular verbs shown gives page numbers where the conjugations of particular tenses are given. These groups are then followed by common verbs—and their definitions—that follow those patterns. By recognizing which common verbs follow a certain pattern, you will greatly increase your vocabulary—all at a glance.

Regular Verbs

Verbs Without Changes in the Stem Ending

Most regular verbs follow the pattern of *machen*. The various conjugations of *machen* can be found on the following pages:

```
present, 8                        present perfect, 23
future, 16                        future perfect, 29
preterite (simple past), 17       present subjunctive, 36, 38
imperative, 34                    past subjunctive, 40
```

Note: The past perfect tense is formed like the present perfect with an auxiliary (*haben* or *sein*) and a past participle. However, the auxiliary is conjugated in the past tense (*hatte gemacht*). (See page 28.) Those verbs that use the auxiliary *sein* are noted in parentheses.

The following list contains common verbs that conform to the pattern of *machen*:

bauen	to build	**führen**	to lead, to guide
blicken	to look, to glance	**glauben**	to believe
brauchen	to need	**glühen**	to glow
decken	to cover	**hauen**	to beat
dienen	to serve	**holen**	to fetch, to get something
drucken	to print	**hören**	to hear
drücken	to press, to push	**kauen**	to chew
erben	to inherit	**kaufen**	to buy
fragen	to ask	**kehren**	to sweep, to turn
fühlen	to feel	**kochen**	to cook

lachen to laugh	**sorgen** to worry
leben to live, to be alive	**spielen** to play
legen to put something into a horizontal position, to lay	**spülen** to wash, to rinse
lehren to teach	**stammen** to originate
lernen to learn	**staunen** to be astonished
lieben to love	**stecken** to put
lügen to tell a lie	**stellen** to put something into a vertical position, to set, to stand
nagen to gnaw	**stimmen** to be right
nicken to nod	**strahlen** to beam, to shine
packen to pack, to seize	**suchen** to look for
regen to move, to stir	**surfen** to surf
reimen to rhyme	**teilen** to share
reisen (sein) to travel	**turnen** to do gymnastics
rücken to move, to shove	**wagen** to risk, to bet, to dare
sagen to say	**wohnen** to live (somewhere)
sägen to saw	**zahlen** to pay
schauen to look	**zeigen** to show
schenken to present, to give as a gift	**zielen** to aim
schicken to send	**zwicken** to pinch
schnallen to buckle, to fasten	

Note: The verbs *fassen, passen,* and *tanzen* also follow the pattern of *machen*. However, the second person singular has only a *-t* ending: *du fasst, passt, tanzt.*

Verbs Ending in *-eln* and *-ern*

Regular verbs with the infinitive endings *-eln* and *-ern* use an *-n* conjugational ending in place of *-en* in the first and third persons plural, for example, *wir basteln* and *sie hämmern*. In all other instances, the conjugation follows the pattern of *machen*. Some verbs that have this variance are:

ändern to change	**kritzeln** to scribble
ärgern to annoy	**lächeln** to smile
basteln to work on a handicraft	**paddeln (sein)** to paddle, to row
behandeln to treat	**plaudern** to chat
betteln to beg	**pudern** to powder
dauern to last	**rudern (sein)** to row
donnern to thunder	**sammeln** to collect
entwickeln to develop	**schaufeln** to shovel
erinnern to remind	**scheitern** to fail
erleichtern to ease	**schmeicheln** to flatter
feiern to celebrate	**schütteln** to shake
flüstern to whisper	**speichern** to store
fordern to demand	**trauern** to grieve
fördern to promote	**verhungern** to starve
füttern to feed	**verprügeln** to thrash, to beat up
hämmern to hammer	**versichern** to insure, to assure
handeln to deal, to trade	**wandern (sein)** to roam, to wander
jodeln to yodel	**wechseln** to change
jubeln to rejoice	**zerschmettern** to smash
klettern (sein) to climb	**zögern** to hesitate
klingeln to ring	

Verbs Ending in *-ieren*

A large category of regular infinitives ends in *-ieren*. Many of these are foreign words to the German language. They follow the pattern of *machen* except that their past participle never has a *ge-* prefix (*studieren: er hat studiert*). Some common verbs to this category are:

arrangieren	to arrange	**klassifizieren**	to classify
demonstrieren	to demonstrate	**komponieren**	to compose
diskriminieren	to discriminate	**marschieren (sein)**	to march
diskutieren	to discuss	**mobilisieren**	to mobilize
elektrifizieren	to electrify	**passieren (sein)**	to happen
existieren	to exist	**probieren**	to try, to taste
explodieren	to explode	**protestieren**	to protest
fixieren	to stare, to gaze	**qualifizieren**	to qualify
fotografieren	to photograph	**spazieren (sein)**	to stroll
funktionieren	to function	**spionieren**	to spy
gratulieren	to congratulate	**telefonieren**	to telephone
imponieren	to impress		

Stem Endings *-t(-)*, *-d(-)*, and *-gn(-)*

Regular verbs with these stem endings are conjugated following the pattern of *arbeiten*. This pattern is similar to the conjugational pattern of *machen* with the exception of an *-e-* added after the stem of the verb and before the conjugational ending (*er arbeitet, er arbeitete, er hat gearbeitet*). The various conjugations of *arbeiten* or similar verbs can be found on the following pages:

present, 9	future perfect, 28
future, 16	present subjunctive, 36
preterite (simple past), 17, 77	past subjunctive, 40
imperative, 34	past participle, 24
present perfect, 24	infinitive, 7

Note: The past perfect tense is formed like the present perfect with an auxiliary (*haben* or *sein*) and a past participle. However, the auxiliary is conjugated in the past tense. (See page 28.) Those verbs that use the auxiliary *sein* are noted in parentheses.

Some of the most common verbs that follow the pattern of *arbeiten* are:

achten	to respect	**fürchten**	to be afraid
antworten	to answer	**heiraten**	to marry
atmen	to breathe	**jäten**	to weed
bilden	to form	**ketten**	to chain
bluten	to bleed	**läuten**	to ring, to toll
dichten	to write poetry	**leisten**	to accomplish
duften	to be fragrant	**leuchten**	to shine, to illuminate
dulden	to put up with, to tolerate	**melden**	to report in
ernten	to harvest	**mieten**	to rent
flirten	to flirt	**neiden**	to envy
fluten	to flood, to flow	**ordnen**	to arrange

reden   to give a speech, to speak
regnen   to rain
richten   to direct, to address
rösten   to roast
schalten   to switch

schulden   to owe
stiften   to found, to establish
töten   to kill
trotten (sein)   to trot along

Irregular Verbs in the Present Tense

Stem-Vowel Change from *e* to *i* or *ie*

Examples of present tense irregularities with a vowel change from *e* to *i* or *ie* are found on the following pages with the verbs *geben* and *sehen*:

> present; 9, 10

Some common verbs with these kinds of vowel changes are:

befehlen   to order, to command
brechen   to break
empfehlen   to recommend
essen   to eat
fressen   to eat (used with animals), to devour
gelten   to be valid
geschehen (sein)   to happen
helfen   to help
lesen   to read
melken   to milk

messen   to measure
nehmen   to take
sprechen   to speak
stechen   to stab
stehlen   to steal
sterben (sein)   to die
treffen   to meet
treten (sein)   to step
verderben   to go bad, to spoil
vergessen   to forget
werfen   to throw

Stem-Vowel Change by Umlaut

An example of a present tense irregularity in the second and third persons singular with a vowel change by umlaut is represented by the verb *tragen* on the following page:

> present, 10

Some common verbs with this kind of vowel change are:

backen   to bake
blasen   to blow
braten   to fry
fahren (sein)   to drive
fallen (sein)   to fall
fangen   to catch

graben   to dig
halten   to hold
laden   to load
laufen (sein)   to run
raten   to advise
schlafen   to sleep

schlagen to hit
stoßen (stößt) to push, to punch, to kick
wachsen (sein) to grow
waschen to wash

Irregular Verbs in the Past Tense

Stem-Vowel Changes

There are numerous verbs that form the past tense in an irregular way. The most common is by the change of the vowel in the stem of the verb. The past tense formations of *schreiben, sehen, fahren, laufen,* and *reißen* occur on the following pages:

> preterite (simple past): 17, 19, 20

Some common verbs that have a vowel change in the past tense and follow the pattern of *schreiben, sehen, fahren, laufen,* and *reißen* are:

befehlen to order, to command
beginnen to begin
beißen to bite
biegen to bend
binden to tie
bitten to request
bleiben (sein) to stay
brechen to break
empfehlen to recommend
essen to eat
fallen (sein) to fall
fangen to catch
finden to find
fliegen (sein) to fly
fliehen (sein) to flee
fressen to eat (used with animals), to devour
geben to give
gehen (sein) to go
geschehen (sein) to happen
gewinnen to win
hängen to hang
heißen to call, to be named
helfen to help
kommen (sein) to come
kriechen (sein) to creep, to crawl
lassen to let
leiden to suffer
lesen to read

liegen to lie, to be situated
lügen to tell a lie
nehmen to take
pfeifen to whistle
reiben to rub
riechen to smell
rufen to call
schlafen to sleep
schneiden to cut
schweigen to be silent
schwimmen (sein) to swim, to float
singen to sing
sinken (sein) to sink, to go down
sprechen to speak
springen (sein) to jump
stehen to stand
stehlen to steal
steigen (sein) to climb
sterben (sein) to die
stoßen to push, to punch, to kick
streiten to argue, to quarrel
tragen to carry, to wear
treffen to meet
trinken to drink
verderben to go bad, to spoil
verlieren to lose
werfen to throw
ziehen to pull

Irregularities in the Perfect Tenses

Irregular Past Participles

In the formation of the present, past, and future perfect conjugations, a past participle is used. Many past participles have an irregular form. The most common characteristic is that most end in *-en* in their past participial forms. The verbs *bleiben*, *sehen*, and *lesen* on the following pages illustrate such irregularities:

> present perfect, 24
> past perfect, 28
> future perfect, 28

These are some common verbs that form an irregular past participle in the perfect tenses and follow the pattern of *bleiben*, *sehen*, and *lesen*. If the auxiliary of the following verbs is *sein*, it is noted in parentheses.

befehlen   to order, to command
beißen   to bite
binden   to tie
bleiben (sein)   to stay
brechen   to break
essen   to eat
fahren (sein)   to drive
fallen (sein)   to fall
fangen   to catch
finden   to find
fliegen (sein)   to fly
fliehen (sein)   to flee
fressen   to eat (used with animals), to devour
frieren   to freeze
geben   to give
gehen (sein)   to go
gewinnen   to win
halten   to hold
laufen (sein)   to run
liegen   to lie, to be situated
lügen   to tell a lie
nehmen   to take
reißen   to rip

reiten (sein)   to ride
rufen   to call
schießen   to shoot
schlafen   to sleep
schließen   to close
schneiden   to cut
schreiben   to write
schweigen   to be silent
schwimmen (sein)   to swim, to float
singen   to sing
sitzen   to sit
sprechen   to speak
stechen   to stab
stehen   to stand
stehlen   to steal
steigen (sein)   to climb
sterben (sein)   to die
tragen   to carry, to wear
verbieten   to forbid
wachsen (sein)   to grow
waschen   to wash
werfen   to throw
ziehen   to pull
zwingen   to force

Modal Auxiliaries

The six modal auxiliaries follow a special conjugational pattern in the various tenses. The modal *können* illustrates this pattern on the following pages:

> present, 14
> preterite (simple past), 21
>
> present perfect, 26, 27
> present subjunctive, 37

The modals form a double infinitive structure in the present perfect tense (p. 26) and in the future tense (*ich werde schreiben können*).

The following modal auxiliaries follow the pattern of *können*. Their singular present and preterite forms are shown:

dürfen (darf, durfte) may, to be allowed
können (kann, konnte) can, to be able to
wollen (will, wollte) to want

mögen (mag, mochte) to like
sollen (soll, sollte) should
müssen (muss, musste) must, to have to

Note: The verb *wissen* also follows this pattern in the present (*weiß*, p. 13) and preterite (*wußte*, p. 22), but its past participle (*gewußt*) cannot be changed to a double infinitive structure like the modal auxiliaries.

Mixed Verbs

Mixed verbs follow a pattern of conjugation in the preterite and present perfect tenses similar to *wissen* (p. 22). They require a vowel change in the stem in the preterite and when forming the past participle. The following mixed verbs conform to this pattern:

brennen to burn
bringen to bring
denken to think
erkennen to recognize
kennen to know, to be acquainted with

rennen (sein) to run
senden to send
wenden to turn

The Verbs *Haben*, *Sein*, and *Werden*

The verb *haben* can stand alone or act as an auxiliary for the perfect tenses. The following pages contain examples of these functions:

> present, 12
> preterite (simple past), 20
> imperative, 47
>
> present perfect, 23, 26
> present subjunctive, 47
> past subjunctive, 40

The verb *sein* can stand alone or act as an auxiliary for the perfect tenses and the passive voice. The following pages contain examples of these functions:

```
present, 12                        present subjunctive, 37, 39
preterite (simple past), 20        past subjunctive, 40
imperative, 35                     passive voice, 42
present perfect, 23, 27
```

The verb *werden* can stand alone or act as an auxiliary for the future tense or the passive voice. The following pages contain examples of these functions:

```
present, 13                        future perfect, 28
preterite (simple past), 20        present subjunctive, 37, 39
present perfect, 27                passive voice, 41
```

Prefixes

Separable Prefixes

Separable prefixes help color the meaning of a verb. Many are formed from direct objects, prepositions, and adverbs, for example: *teil*, *auf*, and *fort*. Examples of the verbs *aussteigen*, *aufpassen*, and *anfangen* can be found on the following page:

```
present, 31                        imperative, 31
preterite (simple past), 31
```

The key to verbs in this category is the separation of the prefix from the verb in the present and preterite tenses and of the prefix from the past participle by -*ge*- in the perfect tenses. Verbs that follow this pattern can be regular or irregular and require the auxiliary *haben* or *sein*.

abfahren (sein) to depart
anziehen to dress
aufmachen to open
aushalten to hold out
ausziehen to undress
beibringen to teach
durchfallen (sein) to fail
einstellen to tune in to
fernsehen to watch television
festhalten to hold on
fortdauern to continue without interruption

heimkommen (sein) to come home	stattfinden to take place
losfahren (sein) to start off	teilnehmen to participate
mitkommen (sein) to come along	umsteigen (sein) to transfer
nachfragen to inquire about	zumachen to close

Inseparable Prefixes

Inseparable prefixes do not change position when a verb is conjugated. They are: *be-, er-, emp-, ent-, ge-, ver-,* and *zer-* (p. 32). The auxiliary of a verb can be changed in the perfect tenses if the prefix changes the verb from intransitive to transitive, for example, *ist gekommen* and *hat bekommen*. Verbs that follow this pattern can be regular or irregular and require the auxiliary *haben* or *sein*.

bedauern to regret	geschehen (sein) to happen
begehen to commit	vergiften to poison
empfangen to receive	verkaufen to sell
empfehlen to recommend	vermieten to lease to someone
entführen to abduct	verpassen to miss out on something
entnehmen to take from	versagen to fail at something
entziehen to move away, to withdraw	versuchen to try
erheben to elevate	zerbrechen to shatter
erkämpfen to win something in a fight	zerfallen (sein) to fall to pieces, to disintegrate
errichten to set up, to build	
erwarten to expect, to await	zerschmettern to smash
erzwingen to get by force	zerstören to destroy
gehören to belong to	zerstreuen to disperse

Separable and Inseparable Prefixes

Some prefixes can be used either as separable or inseparable prefixes. If the accent is on the stem of the verb, the prefix is separable. If the accent is on the prefix, the prefix is inseparable. The most common of these prefixes are *durch-, um-,* and *unter-* (p. 33). Verbs that have these prefixes can be regular or irregular and require the auxiliary *haben* or *sein*.

dúrchfallen (sein) to fail	úmrühren to stir, to agitate
dúrchreisen (sein) to travel through	úmtauschen to exchange
durchsúchen to search through	unterbréchen to interrupt
durchwében to interweave	úntergehen (sein) to go under
umármen to embrace	unterríchten to teach
úmbringen to kill	untersúchen to investigate

Reflexive Verbs

Regular Verbs

Many regular verbs are reflexive. They follow the pattern of *machen* in the various tenses or follow the slight variances for *-ieren* verbs or verbs with the stem ending *-t(-)*, *-d(-)*, or *-gn(-)*. The reflexive pronoun follows the conjugated verb (*er fragt sich*, p. 87). Some of the commonly used reflexive regular verbs are:

sich ändern	to change oneself	sich kleiden	to dress
sich ärgern	to irritate	sich kümmern	to take care of
sich aufregen	to get excited, to get mad	sich leisten	to afford
sich beeilen	to hurry	sich melden	to report
sich beschäftigen	to be occupied, to keep busy	sich nähern	to approach
sich beugen	to lean, to bend	sich rächen	to avenge oneself
sich einbilden	to be conceited	sich rasieren	to shave
sich einigen	to agree	sich schämen	to be ashamed
sich entfremden	to alienate oneself	sich schminken	to put on makeup
sich erinnern	to remember	sich sehnen	to yearn, to long for
sich erkälten	to catch cold	sich setzen	to sit down
sich ernähren	to nourish, to feed oneself	sich sorgen	to be concerned
sich fragen	to wonder, to ask oneself	sich täuschen	to be wrong
sich freuen (auf)	to look forward to	sich trösten	to console oneself
sich freuen (über)	to be glad about	sich überlegen	to consider
sich fühlen	to feel (a certain emotion)	sich umdrehen	to turn (around)
sich gewöhnen (an)	to become accustomed to	sich verabreden	to make a date
sich interessieren	to be interested	sich verabschieden	to say good-bye
sich irren	to go astray, err	sich verlieben	to fall in love
sich kämmen	to comb (one's hair)	sich verständigen	to come to an understanding
		sich vorstellen	to imagine
		sich wundern	to be amazed

Irregular Verbs

Many irregular verbs are also reflexive. They follow the pattern of a vowel change from *e* to *i* or *ie* as illustrated by the verbs *geben* and *sehen* on the following pages:

present; 9, 10

With irregular verbs, the reflexive pronoun follows the conjugated verb (*wir sehen uns*, p. 87).

The irregular past tense of *schreiben, sehen, fahren, laufen,* and *reißen* occurs on the following pages:

past; 17, 19, 20

In the irregular past tense, the reflexive pronoun follows the conjugated verb (*wir sahen uns*).

The most common characteristic of irregular verbs formed as past participles is that most end in *-en* in their past participial form. The verbs *bleiben*, *sehen*, and *lesen* on the following pages illustrate such irregularities:

> present perfect, 24 future perfect, 28
> past perfect, 28

In the perfect tenses and the future tense of irregular verbs, the reflexive pronoun follows the auxiliary (*wir haben uns gesehen, wir werden uns sehen*).

Some common reflexive verbs that have irregularities in the preterite and the perfect tenses are:

sich anziehen   to dress
sich ausziehen   to undress
sich befinden   to be located
sich benehmen   to behave
sich besinnen   to recollect
sich beziehen   to relate, to refer
sich entscheiden   to decide
sich entschließen   to make up one's mind
sich scheiden   to part, to get a divorce
sich streiten   to argue, to quarrel
sich umziehen   to change clothes
sich unterhalten   to converse
sich verhalten   to behave, to react
sich verlaufen   to get lost
sich verschreiben   to make a slip of the pen, a typo
sich vertragen   to get along with
sich vollziehen   to take place
sich vorkommen (sein)   to happen, to seem
sich vornehmen   to plan, to resolve to do something
sich waschen   to wash oneself
sich wenden   to turn to, to contact
sich zurückziehen   to withdraw, to retreat

Notes

Notes

Notes

Notes

Notes

Notes

www.ingramcontent.com/pod-product-compliance
Lightning Source LLC
Chambersburg PA
CBHW071406160426
42813CB00084B/633